TARGET
Maths in Secondary Schools

For Class Teachers, SENCOs and
Support for Learning Staff

Rosemary Baxter and Linda Harrison

Barrington Stoke

First published 2005 in Great Britain by Barrington Stoke Ltd,
Sandeman House, Trunk's Close, 55 High Street, Edinburgh, EH1 1SR

www.barringtonstoke.co.uk

ISBN 1-84299-297-X

Edited by Julia Rowlandson

Designed and typeset by GreenGate Publishing Services, Tonbridge
Printed in Spain

Contents

Who is this Book Designed to Help?

This book is intended for use with students who are not coping well in secondary school, because they have gaps in their understanding and knowledge that make them unable to access the teaching.

A student who is not grasping the basic ideas needs to be taken back to the point where his understanding initially broke down and to review the basics by using methods that are multi-sensory, concrete and practical.

Only once core knowledge has been understood will it be possible to build on this and reintroduce concepts which have been misunderstood and used inaccurately.

To many students, applying mathematical techniques is like being blindfolded and trying to pin the tail on the donkey.

They use skills they do not understand, and work on blind hope. They do not know why they are right or wrong – and they have no idea how to improve their performance.

Many adults who help out or work in classrooms listen to teachers explaining different ideas and techniques. They are known to say how much better they understand what is being taught now than they did when they were at school.

Why is this?

They are able to **listen** without fear of being unable to carry out what is being taught, they are able to **relate** what they do to real life situations, they are **open** to the learning process, they are **confident** enough to ask for explanation.

If we provide a supportive environment where students are able to let go of their fear and open themselves to learning, they, too, will begin to achieve success.

Mathematics: perhaps more than any other subject, depends on the understanding of what has gone before. A student who does not see how numbers fit together in sequence will not understand percentages or ratio: a student who has missed out on weeks of study will not be able to absorb work that depends on teaching he has missed. What is more, for every student, the point of breakdown will be different.

This leads on to another of the causes of trouble with maths: **fear**. Once the subject becomes difficult, a student learns to dread it and believes it is impossible to master. It is not so – but the learner must be prepared to backtrack and ensure that there is a good understanding of the core elements of the subject.

The enemy of true mathematical understanding is the fast pace needed in the classroom to be moving forward continually on a programme of teaching which assumes knowledge of previous learning is secure.

It is counter-productive to concentrate exclusively on the syllabus for exams before being sure that the student has grasped the understanding of the basics.

These basic skills are divided in this book into three areas:

Skills Area 1 depends on understanding the way in which words can be used to give instructions. It involves understanding how numbers relate to each other and what the processes used will do to numbers and why.

Skills Area 2 ensures that students have the essential skills needed to employ their understanding of number relationships.

Skills Area 3 looks at implementing these skills and building on the solid knowledge the student has acquired to apply these to the topics needed for examinations success in the secondary situation.

Dominating any emphasis on skills we have the most vital area of all: **a student has to be ready, willing and prepared to learn.**

It does not matter how well he is taught if he refuses to learn. A student should be shown how to improve his own learning by using strategies that work for him. This involves developing study skills, such as time management, organisation, awareness of learning styles, revision techniques and examination skills.

A student will be able to deal more confidently with maths in the school curriculum when he has:

- a basic understanding reinforced using practical, multi-sensory methods and constant rehearsal,
- knowledge linked into situations where the tasks can be visualised in practical use.

In order to address the issues of motivation and low self-esteem, simple target cards have been included to enable students, teaching assistants and class teachers to recognise progress and reward success.

Behaviours you May have Noticed

Students who are experiencing difficulty with maths may display a variety of symptoms – not the least of which is bad behaviour in lessons. Have you observed any or all of these?

- Fear
- Lack of confidence
- Task avoidance
- Slow processing
- Over-dependence on checking with the teacher
- Errors in basic calculations

- Difficulty with subtraction/division
- Inability to carry out steps in sequence
- Inconsistency
- Lack of understanding of the questions
- Inability to estimate to see that answers are impossible
- Inability to remember
- Inability to transfer learned skills
- Slow speed of working
- Muddled, messy presentation of work
- Disruptive behaviour

These problems will not just apply in mathematics, although they are often more concentrated there. There will be knock-on effects noticeable in science, geography, design and any other subject that uses the same skills.

The Benefits

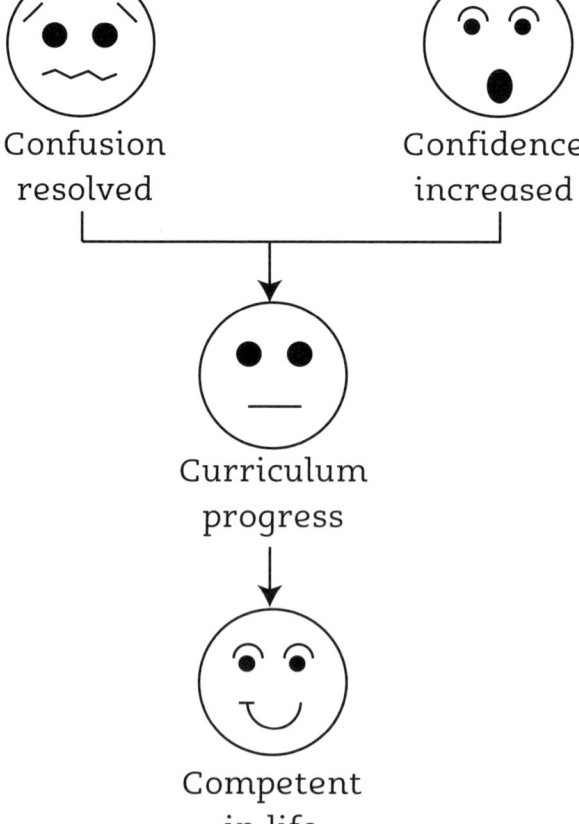

Learning Styles

Not all students learn in the same way. Some people learn best through **seeing**, others learn through **hearing** and the rest need to acquire skills through **doing**. Teaching that involves all methods of learning tends to be most successful. However, **doing** without **understanding** (which can sometimes describe classwork), is unproductive as the student cannot reproduce what he is doing at other times.

Visual learners remember best through using

- Pictures
- Diagrams
- Grouping using colour
- Highlighting and marking text.

Auditory learners benefit from

- Discussions
- Oral explanations
- Reading aloud
- Talking through what they do.

Kinaesthetic learners like to
- Move through a learning pattern
- Be practical
- Use real experiences
- Employ concrete examples
- Making games or models.

Students need to develop an awareness of what style of learning suits them best.

Learning styles and tables

A **visual** learner might find it helpful to colour in the pattern on a number line or in a hundred square. He could put a poster where he sees it frequently, or practise picturing the image when he closes his eyes.

An **auditory** learner might do better if he recites the table out loud, or sets it to music. He might benefit from making a tape – leaving gaps for him to say the answer, then repeating each element as a whole: e.g. three times four equals twelve.

A **kinaesthetic** learner could use counters to build up a physical awareness of how the pattern grows, make models or play a game that uses the skill.

Some activities work with more than one learning style – use a variety of tasks incorporating seeing, hearing and doing.

Inchworms and Grasshoppers

Steve Chinn (*The Trouble with Maths*: 2004, RoutledgeFalmer, ISBN 041532498X) has done a lot of work on looking at the two types of learner in maths

- Inchworms are procedural and like to work systematically through a problem. They like to use learned methods and work mechanically, but are unlikely to check their answer, or see that it cannot be correct.
- Grasshoppers are more impulsive and work intuitively. They often leap straight from problem to answer without detailing how they get there. They will develop short cuts and use their own methods of getting answers.

Some parts of the maths curriculum are more likely to appeal to grasshoppers, (e.g. geometry), whereas others, (such as algebra) are better suited to inchworms.

Repetition

To learn effectively a student needs to reinforce new skills until they become automatic.

Recall is stimulated most effectively when work is repeated or reviewed

- within 24 hours
- after one week
- a week later
- after one month
- at the end of six months.

Around 80% of new learning is lost within 24 hours. Quick review can double retention – and further repetition improves recall still further.

Using a file system

- Get a file with 30 pockets (for a month).
- At the end of the day, make **a brief revision sheet** for work completed that day.
- Place it in the file for the following day.
- The next day **review** the work.
- Place it in the file for the following week.
- A week later, **go over** the topic again.
- Place it in the file for the following week.
- Again, **review** it quickly.
- Place it in the file for the following month.
- You should find, on going over it, that you **remember** the skill.
- Finally, file that piece of work, so that you can review it again at the end of six months.

Some Strategies for Learning

You can use **VARIOUS** methods to help you learn.

Visualise: You have to learn something? Make a picture in your head that links the things you want to remember. The sillier the image, the more likely you are to remember it. Build up a story that ties together the separate items. Imperial measures may still be used. Twelve inches make a foot? Picture a foot made up like a jigsaw puzzle with twelve pieces. Three feet make a yard? Imagine a back yard filled with three enormous feet.

Associate: Link ideas together. 6 + 4 = 10. This is part of a fact family. If 6 + 4 = 10, then 4 + 6 = 10 and 10 – 6 = 4 and 10 – 4 = 6. Knowing one part of an association leads you to realising that you know the rest. Mnemonics are useful for creating links.

For example: **B**rush **O**ff **D**og **M**ess **A**nd **S**oon, (to remind you that calculators work in the order **B**rackets, **O**ther, **D**ivision, **M**ultiplication, **A**ddition, **S**ubtraction.)

Repeat: Go over information. Start just after you have first learned it and repeat at intervals until it has sunk into your long-term memory. No-one remembers everything the first time they look at it.

Interest: Make it fun. Make it unusual. Use different techniques to learn – if you are bored, you will not remember it. If you feel good about what you are learning, you will be successful.

Organise: Break what you want to learn down into small, bite-sized pieces. Identify what you know already and decide what you want to learn. Do not try to do too much at once and spread your learning out over time.

Understand: You cannot learn what you do not understand. If you realise that you have not made sense of something you have to learn, get help!

Share: You do not have to do it on your own! If you work with friends, teach each other elements of the skills you want to acquire, you will learn more effectively and enjoy it at the same time.

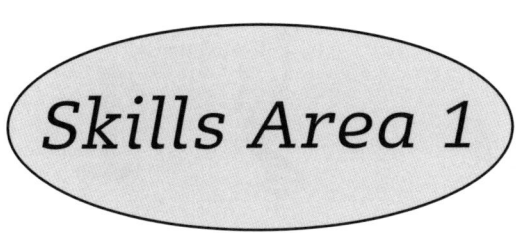
Skills Area 1

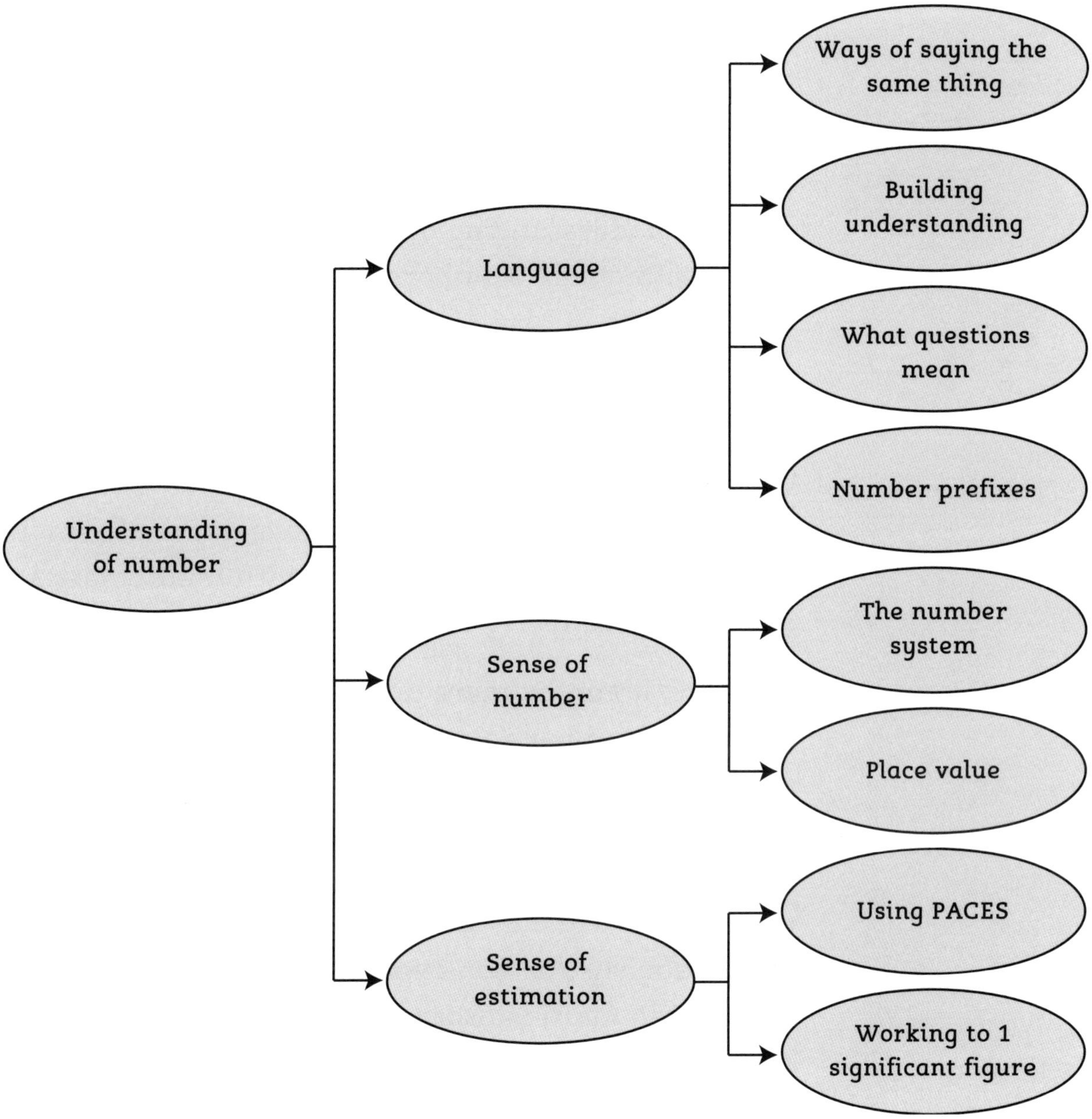

```
                                              ┌─────────────────────┐
                                         ┌───→│ Ways of saying the  │
                                         │    │     same thing      │
                                         │    └─────────────────────┘
                                         │    ┌─────────────────────┐
                                         ├───→│     Building        │
                                         │    │   understanding     │
                            ┌──────────┐ │    └─────────────────────┘
                       ┌───→│ Language │─┤    ┌─────────────────────┐
                       │    └──────────┘ ├───→│  What questions     │
                       │                 │    │      mean           │
                       │                 │    └─────────────────────┘
                       │                 │    ┌─────────────────────┐
                       │                 └───→│  Number prefixes    │
                       │                      └─────────────────────┘
  ┌────────────────┐   │   ┌──────────┐       ┌─────────────────────┐
  │ Understanding  │───┼──→│ Sense of │──┬───→│   The number        │
  │   of number    │   │   │  number  │  │    │     system          │
  └────────────────┘   │   └──────────┘  │    └─────────────────────┘
                       │                 │    ┌─────────────────────┐
                       │                 └───→│    Place value      │
                       │                      └─────────────────────┘
                       │   ┌──────────┐       ┌─────────────────────┐
                       └──→│ Sense of │──┬───→│    Using PACES      │
                           │estimation│  │    └─────────────────────┘
                           └──────────┘  │    ┌─────────────────────┐
                                         └───→│   Working to 1      │
                                              │ significant figure  │
                                              └─────────────────────┘
```

Skills Area 1
Understanding of Number

Before a student can become confident at maths, he needs to have

- An understanding of the language involved in dealing with numbers.
- A sense of how numbers relate to one another.
- A sense of what **will** happen to numbers once various processes are carried out.

When working with students in secondary schools, it is easy to assume that the foundations are well established. In students who have difficulties with mathematics, **this assumption is nearly always wrong**.

However, it can be more difficult to use concrete methods to display number relationships and to encourage the student to vocalise his understanding, since he has learned to conceal his areas of weakness and will feel self-conscious about displaying them. He is likely to be reluctant to use aids which his fellow students might look on as babyish. You can overcome this by involving all students in multi-sensory learning and using **kinaesthetic**, **visual** and **auditory** methods of learning.

Whatever materials are used, it is necessary to cover ideas that go right back to the beginning of mathematical understanding to ensure that the foundation is solid.

Then teach the student to become a **STUD!**

See
Talk
Understand and
Do

(*See photocopiable resource sheet 9*)

The Language of Maths

What is the problem?

A student can have a range of difficulties in understanding the language he is presented with in maths.

- He does not understand the variety of ways in which the same task can be expressed. For example: *the sum of, find the total, add, one number and another* – are all ways of telling a student to add. It often seems that the more difficult a student finds a task, the more ways there are of giving the instructions. **This is not helpful.**
- He might have some difficulty in relating words and symbols, or become confused between similar sounding words, such as eighteen and eighty. In addition, when eighteen is said aloud, he hears the eight (8) first, but in fact needs to write the (1) – so even the recording of the number can confuse him.
- He might not recognise mathematical conventions, such as 0.83 is said as nought point eight three, or regularly misapply language, as in 81 ÷ 9, said as eighty one into nine.
- He cannot decode the instructions to work out what he is being asked to do. This is particularly difficult in long examination questions that tell a story – (often badly!) – and involve several processes.

What does the student need?

First, check that a student **understands** the meaning of different instructions. Then, help him develop **strategies** to remember them. Give him **ways of accessing** what he has forgotten without having to return to the teacher each time.

Where to start

- Create cards that are colour coded to group instructions into families.
- Build up a glossary of terms, which a student explains *in his own words*, so that he has to use it to check what words and symbols mean.
- Develop confidence in **visualising** problems and picking them apart to identify the steps to be taken. **See** the task, **talk** through the steps needed, **understand** what to do and then **do** it!

Ways of saying the same thing

Colour code the different groups – perhaps green for add and red for subtract – this acts as a memory hook and will help a student make links between the different ways of saying the same thing.

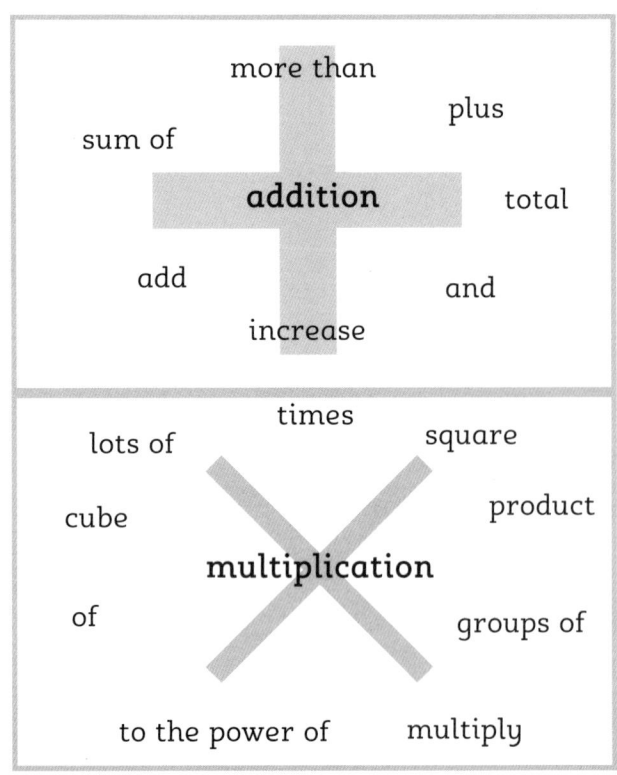

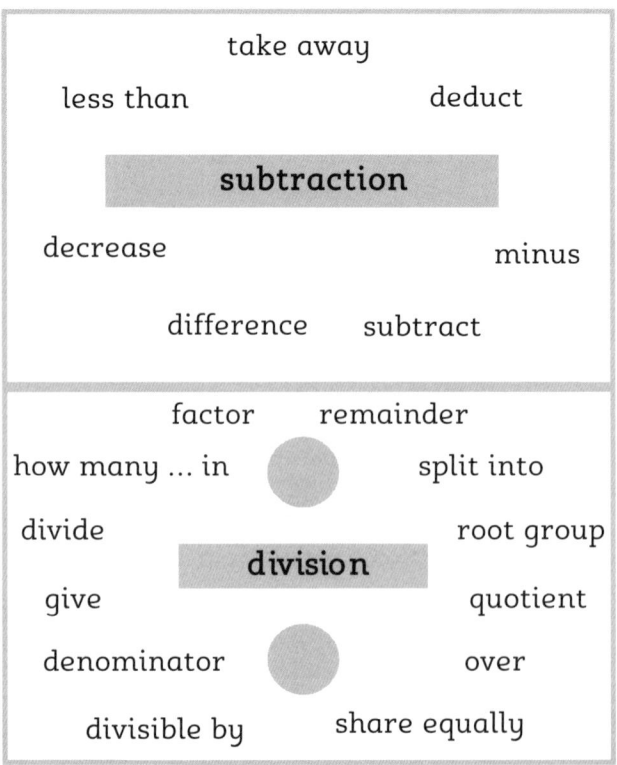

12

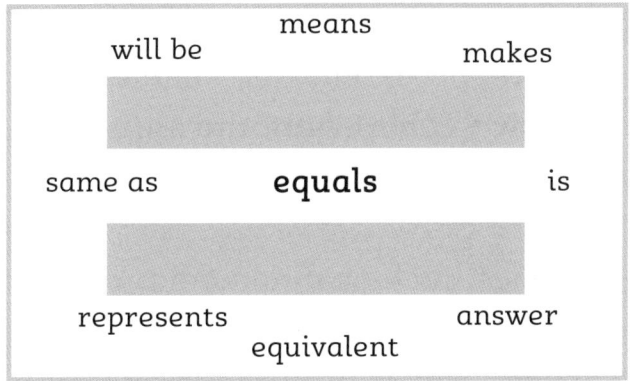

will be
means
makes

same as   **equals**   is

represents
equivalent
answer

Whenever you come across a *different* way of telling you to add, subtract, multiply or divide, put it on your chart.

Building understanding

To help students understand what is **meant** by the terms used in maths

Do:

- Make sure the meaning of mathematical language is explained regularly. Go back over terms used in previous topics. Games or quizzes could be used. (Students could use hundred squares to identify **prime** numbers, or to find **multiples** or **factors** of a number, see page 110)

- Display posters or charts that can be referred to easily, so a student can check without embarrassment. They could include glossaries, posters of shapes with names, formulae, mnemonics, examples of techniques, conversion charts and so on. (See *photocopiable resources 8–10*.)

- Ensure that students keep glossaries of mathematical terms, with examples, filed alphabetically, so they can find them at need. A sheet can be posted in the front of their book giving general terms as well as those needed for the current topic. (See page 15: Making a Glossary.)

- Teach students to highlight in different colours the stages involved in solving wordy problems. Have them practise noting down the stages needed to carry out a task, *without actually performing them*, to accustom themselves to thinking their way through problems.

- Teach the significance of prefixes, see pages 18 and 19, such as milli-, centi-, deca-, kilo-, etc. and ensure the student knows how to abbreviate the units. For example: millimetres = mm, kilogram = kg, centilitre = cl.
- Use memory techniques, such as mnemonics or visualisation to help the student remember horizontal and vertical. This is useful for reading tables and axes in graphs and plotting co-ordinates. (Point to the horizon to find the horizontal, or walk across the hall to find the x axis. Note: if there are only two options, being certain of *one* is enough.)
- Encourage the student to explain to you what he understands.

Never assume that a student understands completely what he is being asked to do. Check by asking him to explain the task back to you – or to a friend. Do not assume that a 'real-life' problem will be easier for a student to understand. These must be carefully thought out – **his** experience of 'real-life' may well not include the elements of the problem and may, indeed, just make it more confusing.

This question asks for knowledge of mathematical language (expression), but it also assumes that a student understands adult references.

Carlos is paid £350 for a 37 hour week and he is paid overtime at a rate of £10 an hour up to 42 hours a week. Any further overtime is paid at time-and-a-half.
One week he works 48 hours. Write an expression that shows how much he will be paid.

What is overtime?   What is time-and-a-half?   What is an expression?

This kind of problem does not really relate to the life experience of most students!

Making a glossary

- Take a set of 25 record cards. (y and z can share a card.)
- Put a letter of the alphabet in the top right-hand corner.
- When a new word is introduced,
  - write the word and highlight it to make it stand out
  - write the meaning in words you understand and
  - give an example or draw a picture.
- File the cards in a box or a small pocket file.
- When a card is full, add another card for that letter.

As words are added to the cards when they are first encountered, they will not be in exact alphabetical order, but they will be easy to find.

For example:

A

Angle There are 4 different types of angle.

acute: less than 90°
right angle: 90°
obtuse: more than 90° and less than 180°
reflex: more than 180° and less than 360°

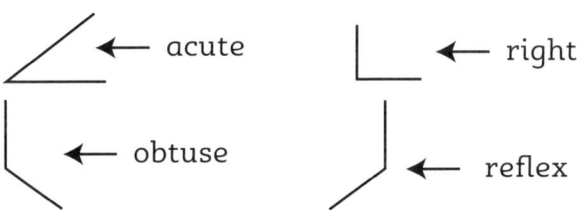

Algebra Maths where letters are used to represent numbers

e.g. $y + 4 = 6$

Anticlockwise The opposite direction to the way the hands of a clock go.

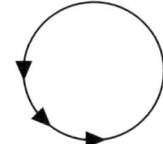

What questions mean – what would you do?

You do not have to find answers to these questions! Your task is to **identify what operations you would have to use to find the answer:** + − × ÷

You can work with a friend.

example

148 students are going to a museum. A coach has 56 seats. How many coaches will be needed for the trip?

To do this I must share 148 out into groups of 56. I must remember that I cannot book part of a coach.

÷

1 Pumpkins are £2.57 each. Carrots are 78p per kilo.

   a) How much does a pumpkin and a kilo of carrots cost? ☐

   b) Carol buys three pumpkins. How much would she spend? ☐

   c) If she buys three pumpkins, how much change does Carol get from a £10 note? ☐

   d) Bananas are £1.99 a kilo. Can Carol buy three pumpkins and a kilo of bananas with her £10 note? ☐

2 Michael, Jason and Allison are in a quiz team. They win £540 in a national competition. They share the money equally. How much does each of them get? ☐

3 In a sale, Ahmed buys a DVD player at half price. If it cost £128 before the sale, how much does he pay? ☐

4 What is the difference between 84 and 23? ☐

5 Six people split £120 equally. How much does each get? ☐

6 What is the product of four and five? ☐

What questions mean – what would you do?

You do not have to find answers to these questions! Your task is to **identify what operations you would have to use to find the answer:** $+ - \times \div$

You can work with a friend.

example

Carton A of juice contains 1 litre of juice and costs 98 p, but Carton B contains 500 ml of juice and costs 61 p. Which is better value?

I need to work out how much they would cost if they were the same size. 500ml is half a litre, so if I multiply that by two, it will tell me how much a litre would cost. Then I can compare the prices. ☒

1. To make concrete cement, sand and water are mixed in the ratio – cement: sand: water = 1 : 3 : 2. How much sand would be needed if there was 3 kg of cement? ☐ ☐ ☐

2. Evaluate ½ + ½ ☐

3. Write ½ as

    a) a decimal ☐

    b) turn the answer to a percentage. ☐

4. Simplify: $3y + 2y + 8y - y$ ☐ ☐

5. Triangle ABC is a scalene triangle.

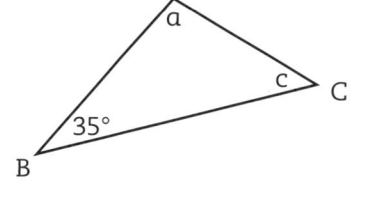

    Angle c is 45° What is angle A? ☐ ☐

6. Deduct 24 from 99. ☐

7. A cube has sides of 6 cm. What is the volume of the cube? ☐

Number prefixes

It is useful to know these number prefixes if you want to understand more words and to know how many sides a shape has.

prefix	meaning	example
mono, uni	one	monorail, unicycle
bi, di	two	bicycle, dioxide
tri	three	triangle
quad	four	quadrangle
quint, pent	five	quintet, pentagon
hex, ses, sex	six	hexagon, sestet
hept, sept	seven	heptagon, septet
oct	eight	octagonal
non	nine	nonagon
dec	ten	decagon

Use **images** to link numbers and prefixes.

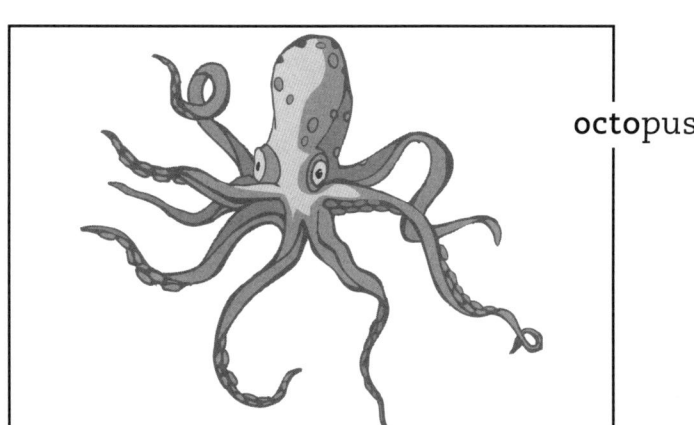

octopus

tricycle

Picture the word on the shape.

Or think of a play on words.

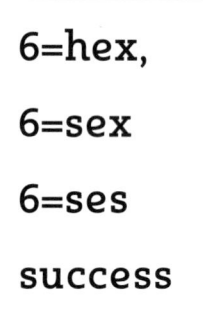

6=hex,

6=sex

6=ses

success

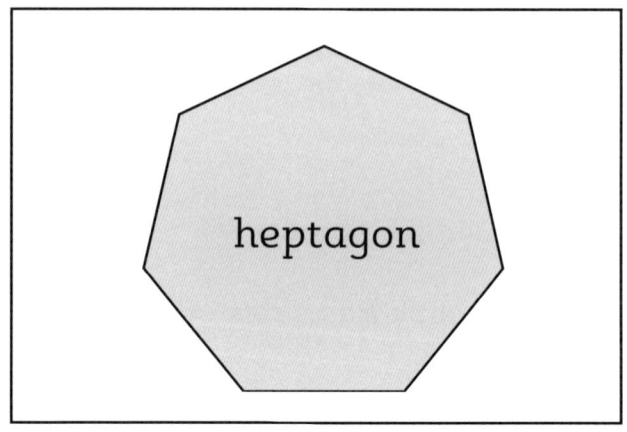

heptagon

Number prefixes

Thousands	kilo	1 kilogram = 1000 grams
Hundreds	hecto	1 hectolitre = 100 litres
Tens	deca	1 decametre = 10 metres
Unit	the unit itself	metre litre gram
tenths	deci	10 decilitres = 1 litre
hundredths	centi	100 centimetres = 1 metre
thousandths	milli	1000 milligrams = 1 gram

There are other number prefixes for millionth, or billion etc. You do not need to know them.

Mnemonic

King Henry Died Unexpectedly Drinking Chocolate Milk

Kilo Hecto Deca Unit   Deci   Centi   Milli

2

Name: _____ Date: _____

TARGET

I can recognise different instructions for multiply and divide.

☐ ☐ ☐ ☐

4

Name: _____ Date: _____

TARGET

I can list the steps needed to work out the answers to problem questions.

☐ ☐ ☐ ☐

1

Name: _____ Date: _____

TARGET

I can recognise different instructions for add and subtract.

☐ ☐ ☐ ☐

3

Name: _____ Date: _____

TARGET

I can read and work out the meaning of problem questions.

☐ ☐ ☐ ☐

---

20   **Target Maths** – Skills Area 1: Understanding of Number

Sense of Number – the Number System

What is the problem?

A lack of understanding of the connections between numbers.

What does the student need?

A student needs to be able to:

Count forwards and backwards
- Count in twos, fives, tens
- Double
- Work with number bonds within ten
- Understand place value
- Understand coin values

Students who can deal with these activities can move on quickly to other tasks.

Many students are not confident enough with the connections between numbers to be able to do away with concrete objects. They need these to help them **visualise** what they are trying to work out.

Materials

These can be helpful –

- Number lines – from 0 – 100
- Hundred squares
- Blank playing cards – these can be grouped easily into bundles of 10, or 100, so that a student can see how place value works. They can be torn into smaller pieces to illustrate fractions or decimals.
- Centimetre tapes and rulers – can be used to provide number lines.
- Triangles of number – reinforce + and – and × and ÷ bonds.

Where to start

Counting forwards and backwards – ones, twos, fives and tens

- Use a number line to count forwards. Start initially with 0 – 20, but later you can use lines that start with different numbers, (even negative ones!).
- The student can use a pencil to show how he is moving.
- Start at the beginning, but move at the student's pace until he can count **from any number** along the line.
- Count first in ones, but move rapidly to counting in twos, fives and tens.
- When the student is confident with the task, introduce counting backwards.

The task can be moved from number lines to working on hundred squares.

Number bonds within 10

Use a grid to check that a student knows that

- different pairs of numbers added together give the same answer
- the order of the pairs can be reversed and still give the same answer
- numbers come in 'fact families'.

10										
1	9									
	2	8								
		3	7							
			4	6						
				5	5					
					6	4				
						7	3			
							8	2		
								9	1	
									10	

Fact families

If $6 + 4 = 10$

then $4 + 6 = 10$ and $10 - 6 = 4$ and $10 - 4 = 6$

Where to next?

Extending fact families to larger numbers

Triangles of numbers can help students who do not have spatial orientation difficulties realise that addition/subtraction and multiplication/division are opposite sides of the same number bonds.

- Take your fact family
- Place the two smaller numbers in the bottom corners of the triangle
- Place the largest number in the top of the triangle
- For subtraction, read from the top: e.g. $23 - 14 = 9$
- For addition, add the two bottom numbers to get the number at the top.
- The same technique can be used with multiplication and division.

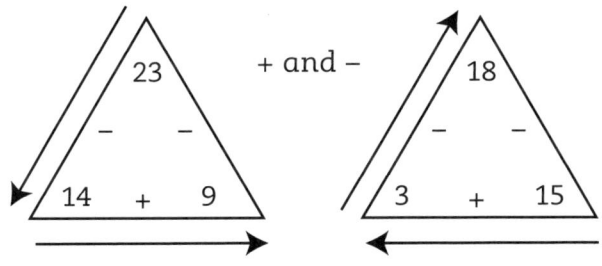

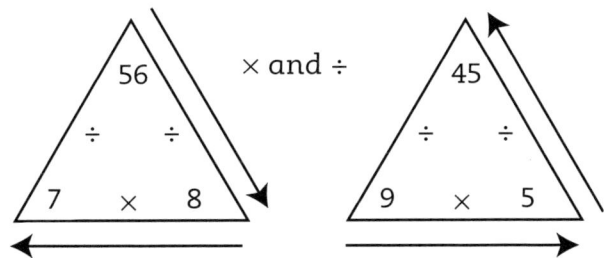

Confidence with fact families helps students understand that numbers are reliable and that they always combine in the same way.

(*Use photocopiable resource sheet 2b*)

Reading and copying accurately

Tip

Many students have difficulty copying numbers from a question. They omit figures or muddle the order. It can help to use a ruler to isolate the number. A set square can be even more useful a tool. If a student lines up the number in the corner of the set square, he can concentrate on one or two figures at a time, and is less likely to make an error. He can move the set square over the number slowly so that only the number of digits he can recall appear with each movement.

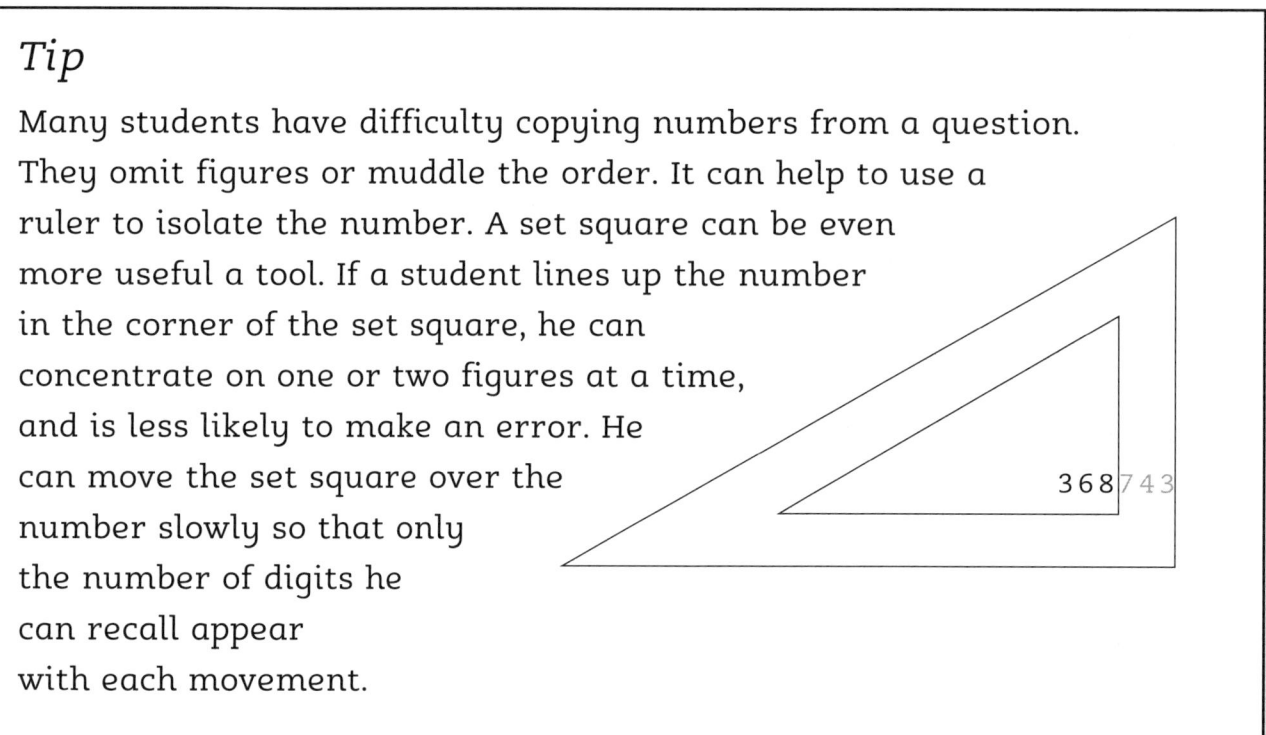

3 6 8 7 4 3

Tip

A set square can also be used to help a student read along the lines of a tables square to read off the answer. It also works as a good tool when reading information from a graph.

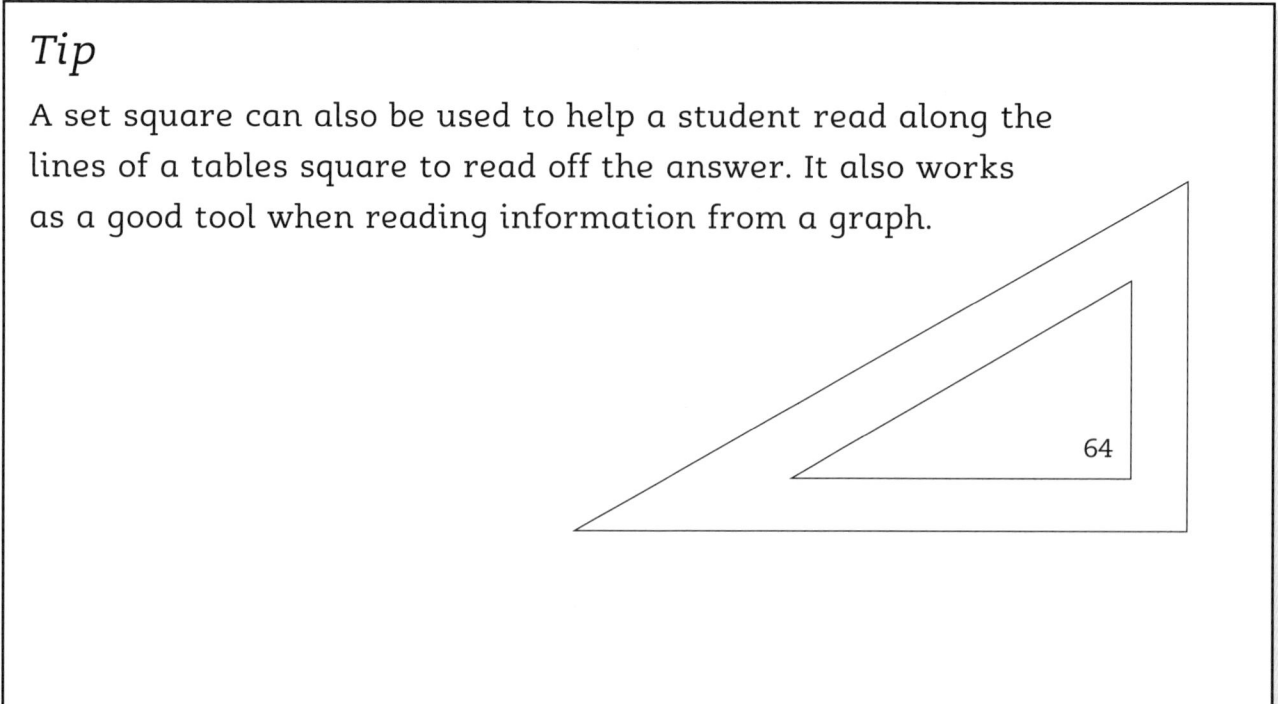

64

Place value

What's the problem? Most teenagers will be able to read and write numbers to 100 and 1000. In fact they may be so familiar with them that it does not occur to them that they do not understand what they mean. They may be very familiar with money and can read and write different amounts but they have no understanding of the significance of the decimal point. Progress in maths is limited if students do not understand place value and the decimal point.

In any part of the maths curriculum there are facts and specialist language which the students need to learn and understand.

Facts

- The difference between a numeral and a number.
- The base of the number system is 10.
- The HTU arrangement, (using whatever terminology is familiar).
- The use of 0 to keep numerals in place.
- In a given number numerals to the left increase in value and numerals to the right decrease in value.
- The decimal point separates whole numbers from parts.

Language of place value

value   increase   decrease   trade   units   tens   hundreds
number   numeral   zero   exchange   tenths   hundredths   digit
thousands   millions

Where to start? Assess the student's understanding of place value.

Getting started

When providing concrete experiences for students it is vital that they are:

- Appropriate for the student's age; many teenagers will be insulted by the use of blocks.
- They should have relevance to their life experiences.
- Ideal materials are ones that can be used in different ways.

The most obvious choice for use with teenage students is money. Sets of money can be purchased from educational catalogues or ask the student to make some.

Assessment activity 1

- Give the student a box of £1 coins and ask him to count them.
- Give the student price tags up to the value of £1000 and ask him to read them.
- Dictate numbers to the student from single digits up to thousands and ask him to write them.

What is the teacher looking for?

Does the student automatically make bundles of ten?

Does the student count in tens?

Does the student read numbers to 1000?

Does the student write numbers to 1000?

Assessment activity 2

Equipment – *Pound coins, £10 notes, £100 notes.*

Give the student a money bank that contains nine £1 coins, nine £10 notes and nine £100 notes.

- Ask him to sort the money out.
- Ask him to write the total amount.

What is the teacher looking for?

Does the student sort the £100 notes in one pile, the £10 notes in one pile and the £1 coins in one pile? Does the student organise the money from left (largest) to right (smallest) in order of value? Can the student write down the total amount?

Assessment activity 3

This can be performed as an activity with teacher observing or as a game.

Equipment – £10, £1 coins, dice marked £0, £1, £3, £4, £5, £6, Place value mat marked with HTU (see photocopiable resources 1b), pencil and squared paper.

To play

1 Set a target, e.g. first person to £50 or £100.
2 Roll the dice, take the amount of money, put the money on the place value mat and then write down the amount on a squared paper.
3 Repeat the activity until the target is reached.

What is the teacher looking for?

Does the student model numbers using the place value mat?

Does the student line up his HTU on the squared paper?

Did the student exchange the £1 coins for £10 notes?

Based on your assessment of the student's understanding, use the suggested activities to give the student risk free, hands-on experiences to develop his understanding of place value.

The activities are planned to:

- give the student some concrete experiences
- give experiences he can visualise

- give opportunities to verbalise numbers (students who have a shaky understanding are very reluctant to read numbers)
- help the student develop strategies to make progress

Activity 1

To help handle equipment and read, speak and write the numbers

Equipment – amount cards *photocopiable sheet 13*, place value chart *photocopiable sheet 1b*, money bank, squared paper.

To start

- Give the student a card with an amount of money written on it.
- Ask him to make that amount on the place value chart.
- Ask him to read it to you.
- Ask the student to write the number on the squared paper.
- Ask him to read what they have written.
- Repeat this activity until he is quick and automatic.

Next

- Teacher to make an amount on the place value chart.
- Ask the student to read it to you.
- Ask the student to write the number on the squared paper.
- Ask the student to read what he has written.
- Repeat this activity until he is quick and automatic.

The student needs to be able to model, read and write numbers automatically, first to 100, then 1000, then 10,000 and so on.

To estimate value

Equipment – place value chart, picture prices, money bank, squared paper.

To start

- Give students pictures of items with a value of less than £100.
- Ask them to use the money bank and to make the amount and put it on the place value chart.
- If playing with two students ask who has the more expensive item.
- If playing with one student ask them to make two amounts and then say which is the more expensive.

Next

If student finds this easy then show him the two value cards and ask which is the *more expensive*. Repeat this activity, asking which is *less expensive*.

To establish value and estimation.

Equipment – number line blanks, amount cards.

To start

- Ask students to make a number line that goes from £0 to £100. They can mark the £50 to give themselves a landmark.
- Give them amount cards and ask them to show you where on the number line the value might be.

cont'd

Moving on

- Give the students two cards.
- Ask them to show you where on the number line the value might be.
- Ask them to say which is bigger or smaller.

Moving further

- Dictate the amounts to the students.
- Ask then to write them on Post-it™ notes and stick them on the number line.
- Ask them to explain to you the value of each.

Activity 4

To establish the process of exchange

Equipment – place value chart, money, amount cards, squared paper.

This can be played individually or as a game.

To start – Set a target, e.g. first one to £100.

- Students take cards indicating amounts.
- They take the amount written on the card from the bank.
- They place their money on the place value chart.
- They write down how much they have.
- They repeat the process and add money to their place value chart. They may need to exchange some of their money to find the most efficient way of representing it. They must read, add and then write down their new total.

At this stage the student should be establishing the golden rule of the system that as soon as there are more than 9 you move up a column.

Activity 5

Moving on to bigger numbers.

The activities 1 to 5 above need to be repeated using bigger numbers. The students tend to have difficulty reading tens of thousand and hundreds of thousand, so extra practice is useful. One million pounds is a great target!

Moving on: Once the students are comfortable reading, writing and modelling numbers, the next stage is to get them to move in two directions. Up to this point, they have increased the amount by moving to the left on the place value mat. Now reverse some of the activities: e.g., start with £100.00 and make the target the first one to reach zero.

Activity 6

Reducing amounts game

This is played in exactly the same way as **Assessment Activity 3** except that the student starts with the target number and has to try to get to 0.

Moving to the decimal point

To start: Give the students an amount of money less than £1000.

- Ask them to put it on their place value chart.
- Ask them what happens as they move up or down the chart.
- Give them a 10p coin and ask them where they will put it.
- Give them a 1p coin and ask them where to put it.

We are trying to use their understanding of the place value chart to extend their knowledge rather than introducing the decimal point as a new concept.

The student's knowledge of exchange can be extended further by repeating **Assessment Activity 3**, page 27. This time use a bank made of 1p and 10p coins. Use a dice marked with 1p 2p 5p 10p 20p 25p. Set the target amount as £1 and play in the same way as before.

Moving on: There are three more things to address.

- Using numbers without the £ sign so they can transfer their learning.
- Reading and showing some of these amounts on a calculator.
- Applying what they have learned to questions in a class text.

The student should now be able to:

Read and write numbers to 1000.

Model numbers using money to 1000.

Give the place value of any digit in a four digit number.

TARGET

Name: _____ Date: _____

1

I can count forwards and backwards in ones, twos, fives and tens.

☐ ☐ ☐ ☐
☐

TARGET

Name: _____ Date: _____

2

I can use triangles to build up number fact families.

☐ ☐ ☐ ☐
☐

TARGET

Name: _____ Date: _____

3

I can deal with whole numbers using hundreds, tens and units.

☐ ☐ ☐ ☐
☐

TARGET

Name: _____ Date: _____

4

I understand place value in whole numbers over 100.

☐ ☐ ☐ ☐
☐

Sense of Estimation using PACES

What is the problem?

Many students have difficulty in coming up with answers close to the truth, because, as far as they are concerned, maths **does not make sense**. It is just that they have very little feel for number.

What does the student need?

The student needs to develop a strategy for working out what a question is asking him to do and what would be a likely answer to that question.

Visualisation can be very useful when confronted with the kind of extended, 'real life' problems so popular in exams. If the student can 'see' in his mind what the whole problem is asking, he can break down the task into a series of stages that will lead to the answer.

So, if a student can

Picture	the problem as a whole – what is it about?
Analyse	the task – what steps do you need to take?
Consider	the steps to carry out each part of the task.
Estimate	what would be a likely answer.
Solve	the problem. Work out the answer and check it.

(*see photocopiable resource sheet 10*)

Developing a systematic habit of going through his **PACES** can help a student improve his accuracy by stopping him from beginning impulsively to make marks on paper before he is sure of what he is doing.

Once a student has begun wrongly, he finds it very difficult to rectify his errors.

It is far better for him to take more *time* to ensure that he knows what to do before he starts.

Where to start

Do:

- Make sure that the student understands the language of estimation.

Necessary terms

guess how many …   nearly   roughly about   to the nearest 10 or 100
estimate   approximately   about the same as   just over   just under
exactly   too few   too many   round up

- Start with the student and ask him to use the language of estimation to talk about himself.

  How old is he? almost/roughly/nearly/about/exactly
  How tall is he?
  How far does he live from school?
  How many CDs does he have?
  How much time does he spend watching television a week?

- Begin with a task that asks a student to estimate number.

  How many sweets in a packet?
  How many bricks in a wall?
  How many steps in a flight of stairs?
  How many pieces of pasta in a jar?
  How many people in a room?
  How many books on a shelf?

- Extend this to ask a student to estimate number of more than one thing.

  If there are about 20 sweets in a packet, how many will there be in five packets?
  If there are about 16 steps in a flight of stairs, how many will there be in 10 flights of stairs?
  If there are 50 books on that shelf, how many will there be on all those shelves? Try to point at an example for a student to see.

- Move on to tasks that ask a student to work out rough answers involving sums of money. Teach the value of rounding to the nearest number that is **one figure and zeros** – (one significant figure).

39p and 81p – more than £1 or less?	(40 + 80)
89p and 52p – more than £1 or less?	(90 + 50)
£3.99 and £7.96 – more than £10 or less?	(£4 + £8)
£68 and £21 – more than £100 or less?	(£70 + £20)

Where to next?

- Extend to making reasoned approximations – or guesses – of answers to questions.

The student starts by **imagining** what the problem is asking and **thinks** about it. This can help with computational tasks such as 723 – 489.
Think 'nearly 500 away from a bit over 700' is going to lead to an approximate answer of 200.
Extend that a stage further to think 'ten less than 500 away from twenty more than 700' is going to give a more accurate estimate of 230.
Once the student knows that the answer will be 'a bit over 200' or 'around 230', he has a standard against which he can check his answer.

This technique does not guarantee accurate answers, *but it helps*. The student uses the feel for number he is developing to decide whether his answer is possible. This is especially important when using a calculator – as a single slip of the finger will give the student the wrong answer.

Try using this system to get a student to break down his task and produce an answer.

What operation?   Rough estimate   Actual answer

Roughly what is the answer?

You do not have to find answers to these questions – yet! Your first task is to try to decide which operations you would use and then to **give a rough estimate of the answer, starting with one figure + zeros.**

example

Example: What is 398 + 232?

Operation	Estimate	Answer

Well, I would say that
398 is almost 400,
232 is close to 200,
400 + 200 is 600.

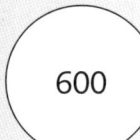

The answer is about 600.

Operation	Estimate	Answer

1 What is 489 + 217?

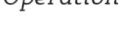  

2 What is 391 + 62?

 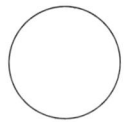 

3 What is 682 – 304?

 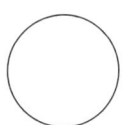 

4 What is the product of 24 and 98?

5 How many times does 29 go into 6015?

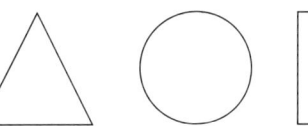 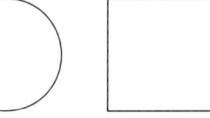

Cont'd

	Operation	Estimate	Answer

6 Four friends share £1994 equally. How much does each get?

△ ◯ ☐

7 Henry buys two books at £2.99 each and a jigsaw puzzle at £2.98. How much does he spend?

△ ◯ ☐

8 There are $1.97 to £1.00. I change £49 into dollars ($). How many will I get?

△ ◯ ☐

9 Mr. Henderson drove 312 miles at an average speed of 48 miles per hour. How long did it take him to reach his destination?

△ ◯ ☐

Extra task:

Now go back and use your calculator to work out the actual answers. Write them in the square. How close was your estimate?

Roughly what is the answer?

You do not have to find answers to these questions – yet! Your first task is to decide what operations you would use and **give a rough estimate of the answer, using one figure + zeros.**

example

Example: Kate saves £19.60 on a dress she buys in a sale. The original price was £78.99. What does she pay?

£78.99 is almost £80.00.
£19.60 is almost £20.00.
£80.00 take away £20.00

Kate will pay about £60.

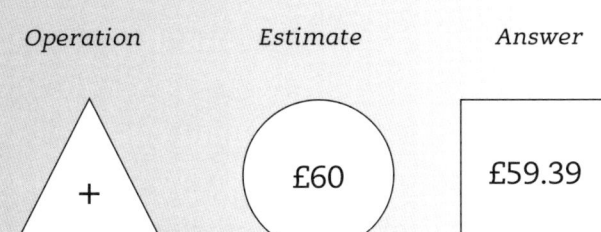

	Operation	Estimate	Answer
	+	£60	£59.39

		Operation	Estimate	Answer

1 How many 29s in 3132?

2 John has 39 CDs, which cost £9.50 each. Roughly how much has he spent on CDs?

3 What is the total of £86.42, £43.10 and £28.50?

4 Ali had £150. He spent £38.99, £62.35 and £12.99. How much does he have left?

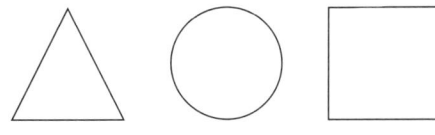

Cont'd

Operation	Estimate	Answer

5 Estimate the answer to
9.67 × 8.099

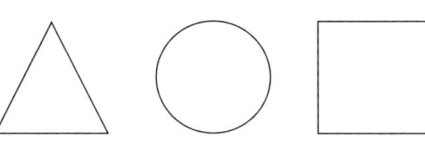

6 A car cost £7899. After the first year it is worth £1479 less. What is it worth now?

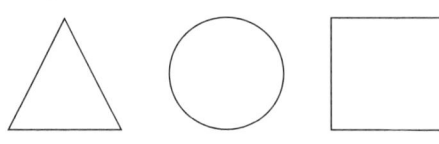

7 The total number of marks a class scored in its examinations was 3895. There are 21 people in the class. Roughly what was the average mark?

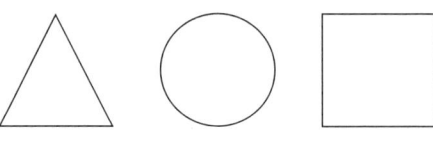

8 There are 20 girls in the model railway club, but there are 2.8 times as many boys. How many boys are in the model railway club?

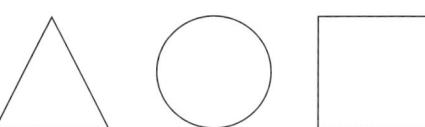

Extra task:

Now go back and use your calculator to work out the actual answers. Write them in the square. How close was your estimate?

TARGET 1

Name: _____ Date: _____

I can estimate the answer to addition problems.

☐ ☐ ☐ ☐

TARGET 2

Name: _____ Date: _____

I can estimate the answer to subtraction problems.

☐ ☐ ☐ ☐

TARGET 3

Name: _____ Date: _____

I can estimate the answer to multiplication problems.

☐ ☐ ☐ ☐

TARGET 4

Name: _____ Date: _____

I can estimate the answer to division problems.

☐ ☐ ☐ ☐

Target Maths – Skills Area 1: Understanding of Number

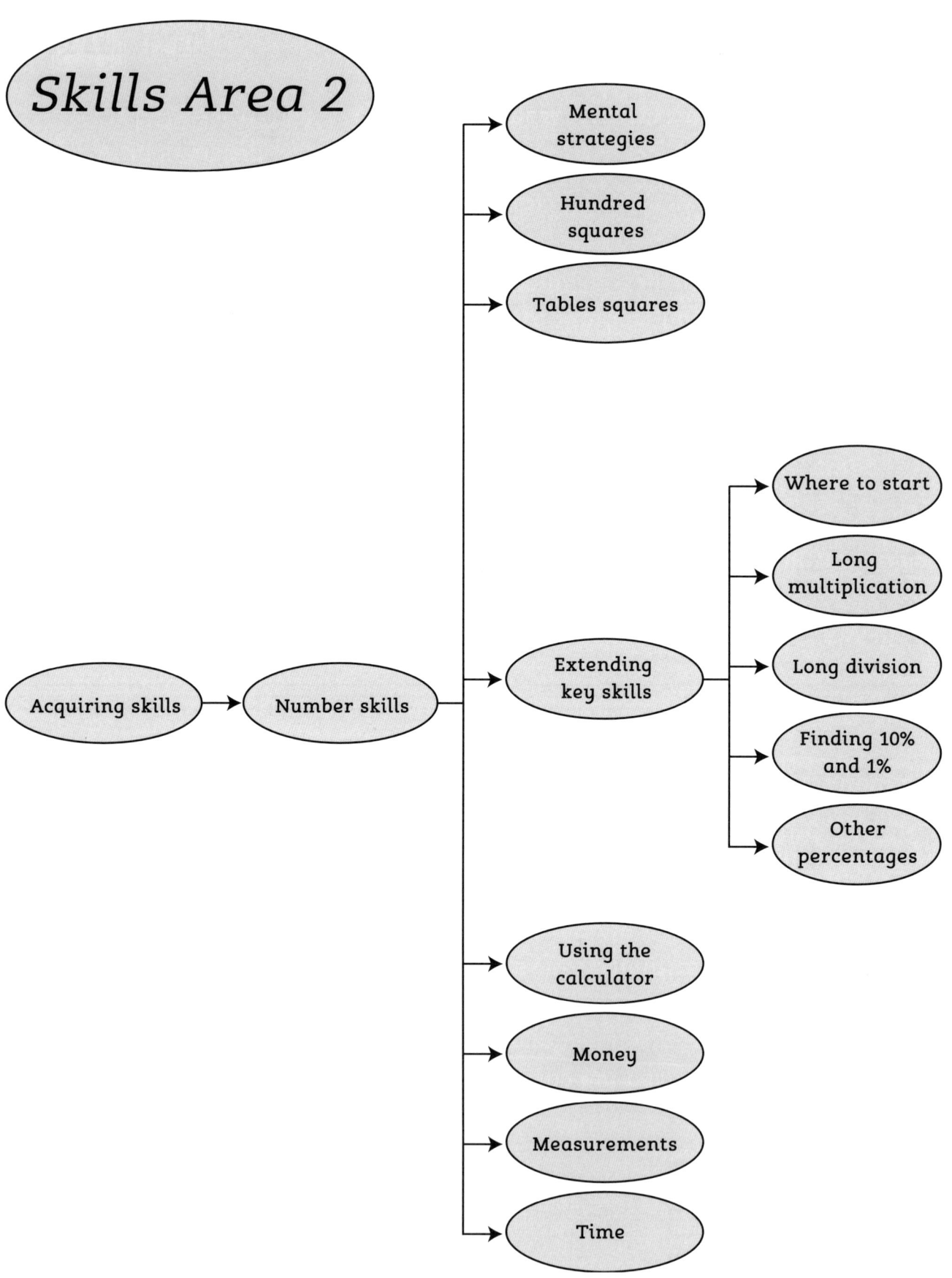

Skills Area 2

Acquiring skills → Number skills

Mental strategies

Hundred squares

Tables squares

Extending key skills
- Where to start
- Long multiplication
- Long division
- Finding 10% and 1%
- Other percentages

Using the calculator

Money

Measurements

Time

Skills Area 2
Acquiring Skills

An essential part of dealing with maths in the secondary curriculum is having the core number skills. A teacher needs to work out what the problem is and then pinpoint the exact needs of the student and where his understanding breaks down. A student needs to feel confident on paper with:

- Addition, including carrying
- Subtraction, including decomposition and dealing with zeros
- Simple multiplication, including tables
- The processes involved in long multiplication
- Simple division within tables
- Long division
- All of the above including the decimal point.

He needs to be able to carry out simple mathematical calculations in his head, and feel confident with rough estimation, so that he can:

- Break down and add two figure numbers
- Break down and subtract two figure numbers
- Multiply and divide whole numbers within his times tables
- Work out 10%
- Using 10 to add 11 and 9
- Using 10 to subtract 11 and 9
- Break down and understand the language of questions.

In addition a student needs to feel confident when dealing with money, which includes the use of the decimal point, and in using measurements such as he will encounter in everyday life. For example:

- Recognise that £4.50 and 87p are in different units and be able to change pounds to pence and pence to pounds.
- Know roughly how long 1 cm, 1 m, and 1 km are.
- Know roughly how much 1 g and 1 kg are.
- Know roughly how much 1 litre is.
- Understand 0°C, 20°C and 100°C.

Visualisation is a very useful way to develop this awareness.

Ice is 0°C.   A warm room is 20°C.   Boiling water is 100°C.
The top joint of your finger is about 2 cm.   A long step is about 1 m.
A bag of crisps is about 25 g.   A bag of sugar is 1 kg.
A bottle of orange squash is 1 litre.   A big bottle of cola is 2 litres.

The student can relate these known reference points to the tasks he pictures:

If **centimetres** measure small things like fingers, he will not use them to state the distance from London to Edinburgh.

If water boils at **100°C**, a metal pan needs to be a lot hotter than that before it will begin to melt.

A useful skill to acquire at this stage is the efficient use of a calculator. It cannot be used to replace mathematical knowledge – but it helps a student avoid simple mechanical errors and can be used to check accuracy and reinforce estimation.

Once a student has a good understanding of core number skills, place value, estimation and an understanding of core mathematical language, he is able to progress to manipulating numbers.

Remember that you can use **VARIOUS** methods to help you learn – and that it helps if a student learns to be a **STUD** (photocopiable resource sheets 8 and 9).

Mental Strategies – Adding or Subtracting 9 or 11

Most students who 'have problems with maths' are hesitant to use mental strategies and lack the confidence to apply them.

However one set of strategies that is easy for students to understand and use are those which help with adding or subtracting 9 or 11.

What facts or skills does the student need to have?

- To count up or back in 10
- To count up or back in 1's

What tools does he need?

- He needs to be familiar with and understand his 100 square (*photocopiable resource sheet 3*)

Where to start?

- Start with 9
- Start with addition

Introductory activities

- Oral practice of adding on 1 or adding on 10 to numbers less than 100.
- Give student a 100 square and ask them to add on 9 by counting on.

Tell the student there is a quicker way and demonstrate.... adding on 10 then back 1.

Make two cards to give him a visual prompt..

This may need to be repeated several times, as the student needs to believe that this method is quicker and more reliable. He needs lots of practice.

Activity

To give extra practice
- Give the student a 100 square.
- Give the student a box with another 100 square to cut up.
- Ask him to choose a number at random.
- Tell him to use the 'two-step model' (+10, –1). If necessary, place the prompt cards in front of him.
- Tell him to use the 100 square to get to the answer as quickly as possible.

Moving on

The next step is to ask the student to use the model to add nine but to do it mentally by visualising the number square.

To start
- Start by practising the sub-skills, adding ten or taking away 1 mentally.
- Demonstrate by using the prompt cards and talking aloud your mental processes.

Moving on
- Ask the student to copy you.
- Ask the student to demonstrate to you.
- Ask the student to add nine without 100 square or prompt cards.

This should all happen quickly with the student becoming automatic. It may be that the student needs to verbalise the two step sequence or he can visualise the process.

Where to next?

Once the learning and model of adding 9 has been achieved, you need to investigate with the student if the model can be used for other calculations.

The aim is; to develop strategies for adding and subtracting 9 and adding and subtracting 11. To establish the mental processes the student needs to begin with the prompt cards and the 100 square to establish the 2 step model.

This is summarised below.

+9	−9
-------------------	-------------------
+10	−10
−1	+1
+11	−11
-------------------	-------------------
+10	−10
+1	−1

When the student is confident orally and can model consistently it is time to give practice on the *photocopiable sheets.*

Sheet 2.1a (page 48) is set out to model the two step procedure.

Sheet 2.1b (page 49) is set out for the student to put in his own workings or move straight to the answer.

The first sum is modelled for you.

Adding and subtracting 9 and 11

The first sum is modelled for you.

Adding 9

Question	+10	−1	Answer
14 + 9	24	23	23
23 + 9			
39 + 9			
52 + 9			
78 + 9			
82 + 9			
47 + 9			

Subtracting 9

Question	−10	+ 1	Answer
23 − 9	13	14	14
31 − 9			
68 − 9			
56 − 9			
39 − 9			
92 − 9			
76 − 9			

Adding 11

Question	+10	+1	Answer
23 + 11	33	34	34
17 + 11			
37 + 11			
52 + 11			
78 + 11			
63 + 11			
80 + 11			

Subtracting 11

Question	−10	−1	Answer
37 − 11	27	26	26
44 − 11			
51 − 11			
99 − 11			
60 − 11			
52 − 11			
29 − 11			

Cont'd

Adding 9		Subtracting 9	
Question	Answer	Question	Answer
23 + 9		31 – 9	
33 + 9		45 – 9	
39 + 9		83 – 9	
66 + 9		52 – 9	
73 + 9		95 – 9	
85 + 9		48 – 9	
47 + 9		67 – 9	

Adding 11		Subtracting 11	
Question	Answer	Question	Answer
47 + 11		47 – 11	
33 + 11		33 – 11	
57 + 11		58 – 11	
73 + 11		93 – 11	
41 + 11		64 – 11	
63 + 11		25 – 11	
88 + 11		39 – 11	

Cont'd

Multiplying and dividing by 10 and 100

What is the problem? Dealing with large numbers.

Where to start: A very useful strategy to develop is the confidence to multiply and divide by 10. This is useful when they are asked to find 10% or 1% of a number.

If a student has built up confidence in the meaning of place value, he should not find it difficult to visualise what happens to a number as it becomes ten times bigger or ten times smaller.

A simple tool to help him see what happens to numbers is to fix a strip of **clear acetate** marked with a decimal point onto a sheet of squared card, leaving spaces for strips of paper to pass underneath. (This tool could be used for the questions on the next page.)

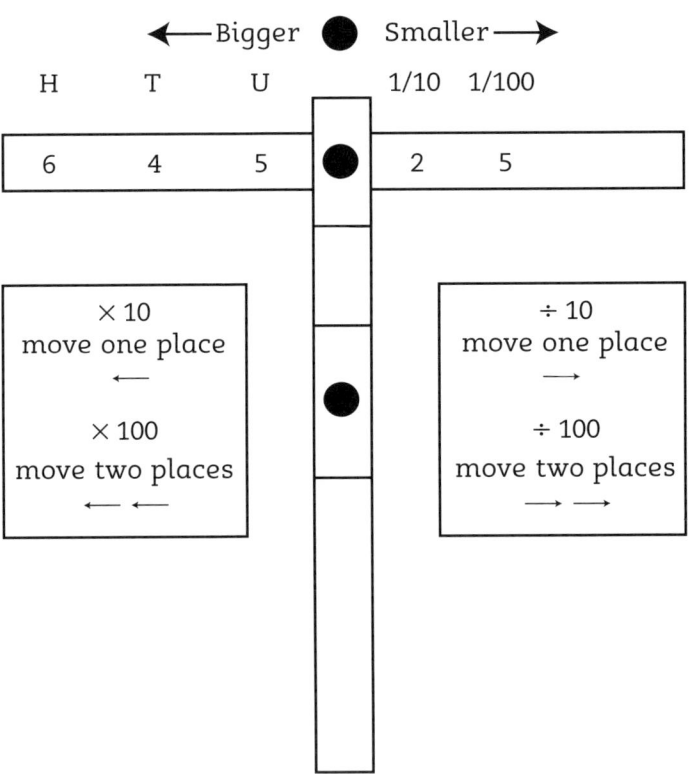

This enables the student to see that the number becomes ten times bigger or smaller.

Students frequently bounce the decimal point to the right when multiplying by ten or a hundred, and move the decimal point to the left to indicate division. This works perfectly well, but gives the impression that the decimal point is moving rather than that the number is becoming larger or smaller. However, if that method works for a student, it is probably best to let him continue with it

---

Where to next:

This skill is particularly useful for finding 10% (see Simple Percentages on page 71)

All this requires a student to do, is divide by ten. Encourage him to visualise the number moving across the decimal point.

10% of £12.50

£1.25

Multiplying and dividing by 10 and 100

Multiplying by 10

Question	Add 0 to the end of the number	Answer
23 × 10	230	230
33 × 10		
3.9 × 10		
66.75 × 10		
73.4 × 10		
85.25 × 10		
47.2 × 10		

Multiplying by 100

Question	Add 00 to the end of the number	Answer
31 × 100	3100	3100
45 × 100		
8.3 × 100		
52.45 × 100		
9.5 × 100		
4.8 × 100		
67.75 × 100		

Dividing by 10

Question	Move decimal point one place to left	Answer
47 ÷ 10	4.7	4.7
33 ÷ 10		
572 ÷ 10		
731 ÷ 10		
4103 + 11		
63.5 ÷ 10		
88.72 ÷ 10		

Dividing by 100

Question	Move decimal point two places to left	Answer
471 ÷ 100	4.71	4.71
332.4 ÷ 100		
58 ÷ 100		
93 ÷ 100		
6.84 ÷ 100		
0.25 ÷ 100		
3.905 ÷ 100		

1

Name: _____ Date: _____

TARGET

I can add on 9 and 11 in my head.

☐ ☐ ☐

2

Name: _____ Date: _____

TARGET

I can subtract 9 and 11 in my head.

☐ ☐ ☐

3

Name: _____ Date: _____

TARGET

I can multiply by 10 and 100 by moving a number across the decimal point.

☐ ☐ ☐

4

Name: _____ Date: _____

TARGET

I can divide by 10 and 100 by moving a number across the decimal point.

☐ ☐ ☐

Target Maths – Skills Area 2: Acquiring Skills 53

Number Relationships – Hundred Squares

What is the problem? A lack of familiarity with number relationships.

Where to start: Hundred squares can be very useful for developing an awareness of patterns in numbers.

1	2	3	4	5	6	7	8	9	10
11	12	13	14	15	16	17	18	19	20
21	22	23	24	25	26	27	28	29	30
31	32	33	34	35	36	37	38	39	40
41	42	43	44	45	46	47	48	49	50
51	52	53	54	55	56	57	58	59	60
61	62	63	64	65	66	67	68	69	70
71	72	73	74	75	76	77	78	79	80
81	82	83	84	85	86	87	88	89	90
91	92	93	94	95	96	97	98	99	100

Game 1

1. Choose a starting point on the square.
2. Give a series of instructions such as 'add 10', '5 less', 'go to 43', '11 more'.
3. The student follows the chain of instruction as quickly as possible.

(If sets of instruction cards are made, a student can play this on his own.)

Game 2

1. Give the student some counters.
2. Ask times tables questions or division within times table questions, such as '10 times 4', 'three nines',

'54 divided by 9', '24 shared between 8', 'the product of 6 and 7'.

3. Work to develop **speed** and **awareness of patterns**.

(When working alone, some students like to use a stopwatch and work against their own fastest speed.)

Students can also use a Hundred Square to identify square numbers, cube numbers, prime numbers, factors and multiples and fractions of one hundred amongst other things.

Where to next: The use of hundred squares can be used to help students develop their confidence with **addition** and **subtraction**.

e.g.　　**32 + 24**

4. Start at 32.
5. Take two steps downwards to add on two 10s.
6. Count on 4 steps to add the units.

(If sets of instruction cards are made, a student can play this on his own.)

e.g.　　**68 – 43**

4. Start at 68.
5. Take four steps upwards to subtract four 10s.
6. Count back 3 steps to subtract the units.

1	2	3	4	5	6	7	8	9	10
11	12	13	14	15	16	17	18	19	20
21	22	23	24	25 ←26 ←27 ←28				29	30
31	32↓	33	34	35	36	37	↑38	39	40
41	42↓	43	44	45	46	47	↑48	49	50
51	52→53→54→55→56					57	↑58	59	60
61	62	63	64	65	66	67	↑68	69	70
71	72	73	74	75	76	77	78	79	80
81	82	83	84	85	86	87	88	89	90
91	92	93	94	95	96	97	98	99	100

Grids

The teacher can quickly make up grids of basic calculations so that the student can practise the technique of adding or subtracting, varying the level of difficulty to match the skill level. Similar grids can be used to practise multiplying and dividing within tables.

e.g.

+	5	4	6	8	2
23					
41					
75					
32					
14					

*Practise using **a hundred square** to add and subtract numbers.*

1	14 + 10 + 6 + 27
2	52 + 14 + 7 + 21
3	23 + 27 + 16 + 24
4	48 + 11 – 20 + 15
5	82 – 61 – 10 + 2 + 22 +37 – 10
6	99 – 33 + 26 + 4 – 17

7 Starting with the top numbers, complete the square.

+	53	25	15	47	61
9					
14					
21					
5					
35					

8 Starting with the top numbers, complete the square.

–	65	82	39	97	53
8					
16					
24					
33					
12					

Multiplication Facts – Tables Squares

What is the problem? Students need to build their confidence as they deal with the variety of processes involved in answering questions in maths. However, students often find it hard to remember tables facts as they are carrying out other tasks. There is no need for them to rely on mental maths memory, **if they develop a strategy for writing down their tables** *before* **they start to work**.

Where to start: Encourage students to spend the first few minutes of every maths lesson writing out a very quick tables square that they can then use for reference throughout the lesson. It helps them understand the process if *they draw up the grid themselves* at first. The inclusion of the zero times table can be omitted when students are confident with the knowledge that anything multiplied by zero is zero.

At first this is more time consuming, but students quickly become more efficient as they realise how useful it is. They also notice that they **know more than they think**. Even those who tell you they cannot do their tables at all will be able to complete three quarters of the square. This only leaves them about half a dozen boxes to fill.

Most students can complete the tables chart to the point shown with little difficulty. Counting on enables them to complete the three and four times tables. By this point they should be aware of the symmetry across the diagonal line made by the square numbers. (Initially it can be helpful to have these numbers entered on an otherwise blank chart.)

x	0	1	2	3	4	5	6	7	8	9	10
0	0	0	0	0	0	0	0	0	0	0	0
1	0	1	2	3	4	5	6	7	8	9	10
2	0	2	4	6	8	10	12	14	16	18	20
3	0	3	6	9	12	15	18	21	24	27	30
4	0	4	8	12	16	20	24	28	32	36	40
5	0	5	10	15	20	25	30	35	40	45	50
6	0	6	12	18	24	30	36				60
7	0	7	14	21	28	35		49	56		70
8	0	8	16	24	32	40		56	64		80
9	0	9	18	27	36	45				81	90
10	0	10	20	30	40	50	60	70	80	90	100

Helpful tables mnemonics for two difficult to remember numbers

- Five, six, seven, eight $\qquad$ $56 = 7 \times 8$
- I **ate** and I **ate** and I was **sick** on the **floor** $\quad$ $8 \times 8 = 64$

This leaves only five numbers to be recalled and three of them are in the 9× table.

Tip

The 9 times table using your hands

Put your hands out flat in front of you. If you bend the **fourth** finger of your left hand, you have **three** fingers to the left of it and **six** to the right. The three fingers represent tens and the six represent units.

$$4 \times 9 = 36$$

cont'd

(Do not nit pick! Thumbs count as fingers here.)

Try it with the ring finger of your right hand, or finger **nine**, counting from the left. You have **eight** fingers to the left and **one** to the right.

$$9 \times 9 = 81$$

Fingers to the left of the target figure are tens, fingers to the right are units – so

$$1 \times 9 = 09$$

that is, no tens and nine units. The same principle operates for 9×10, that is nine tens and no units.

Note: All multiples of nine up to 9×9 **add up to nine.**

In addition the first number is always one less than the number by which you are multiplying. **$3 \times 9 = 27$**

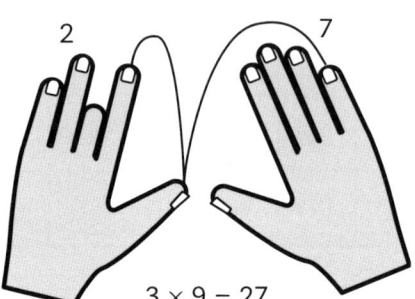

$3 \times 9 = 27$

Tip

Remember that numbers go together in triangles.

If $6 \times 4 = 24$ and $4 \times 6 = 24$, then $24 \div 6 = 4$ and $24 \div 4 = 6$

This means that you can use a tables square to help you with division within the tables.

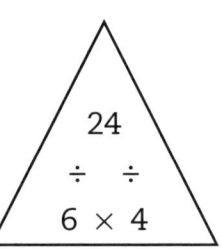

For example: **$71 \div 8$**

Run your finger along the $8 \times$ table until you come to the largest number that is less than 71.

$8 \times 8 = 64$. Therefore 8 goes into 71 eight times with seven left over and the answer is

8 r7 or 8⁷⁄₈

Using the tables square

Before you can work with the tables square, you will need to have one. Although you can keep one handy at most times, in an exam you will need to be ready to make one.

Use a stopwatch to see how quickly you can complete the sheet.

1. Draw and complete a tables square as quickly as you can.

2. Use your tables square to find the answer.

   a) 4×7 b) 8×2 c) 9×6
   d) 7×3 e) 3×5 f) 1×10
   g) 4×4 h) 6×7 i) 2×8
   j) 7×7 k) 9×2 l) 8×8

3. Use your tables square to find the answer.

   a) $54 \div 6$ b) $81 \div 9$ c) $40 \div 5$
   d) $32 \div 4$ e) $27 \div 3$ f) $50 \div 5$
   g) $14 \div 2$ h) $42 \div 6$ i) $72 \div 8$
   j) $63 \div 9$ k) $9 \div 1$ l) $20 \div 2$

4. Use your tables square to find the answer. Write the remainder as a fraction. (Example: $25 \div 4 = 6$ and one over $= 6\frac{1}{4}$)

   a) $37 \div 4$ b) $19 \div 2$ c) $28 \div 5$
   d) $69 \div 7$ e) $41 \div 6$ f) $23 \div 3$
   g) $29 \div 8$ h) $23 \div 10$ i) $31 \div 9$

Now solve these problems:

5. If 36 chocolates are shared evenly among 4 people, how many will each of them have?

6. If nine people are each given £7, how much do they have altogether?

2

Name: _____ Date: _____

TARGET

I am confident that I can complete and use a table square quickly.

☐ ☐ ☐ ☐

4

Name: _____ Date: _____

TARGET

I can use a hundred square to take away a two digit number.

☐ ☐ ☐ ☐

1

Name: _____ Date: _____

TARGET

I can draw up and complete a tables square.

☐ ☐ ☐ ☐

3

Name: _____ Date: _____

TARGET

I can use a hundred square to add on a two digit number.

☐ ☐ ☐ ☐

Key Skills – Pen and Paper Calculations

What is the problem? Before a student can begin to deal with mathematics in the secondary school, he needs to have a grasp of addition, subtraction, multiplication and division that builds on his sense of number. He has generally been taught the techniques, but cannot always apply them.

Where to start

It will help him if he can

- **visualise** what he is doing using an image that means something to him – such as money
- **use concrete examples** and employ counters, pieces of paper, cubes and written examples with small numbers so that he can see how the numbers interact
- **learn to use physical patterning** by moving through a technique in a ritualistic way. Like dancing, swimming or riding a bicycle, if you learn to perform a task in a certain way, you know what to do once you have started.

Be aware that *students with difficulties in maths have often learned to carry out a task by rote (inchworms) or have developed their own strategy (grasshoppers).* Insisting that students use your own different method may well not work and could confuse them, so that they will not be able to use either technique. It is worth watching them use their method, discover where it breaks down and **help them develop a better understanding of their preferred way of working.**

Long multiplication

What is the problem? Long multiplication involves a variety of tasks that need to be carried out in order, including an understanding of place value, memory of tables and addition. It can cause overload.

Where to start: If a student uses a pre-prepared tables square so he can check his tables, the main problem often seems to be in recognising that the figure 4 in 453 is in the hundreds column, so that it actually means 400.

It can help to show the breakdown of the task. 638×453 can be carried out as separate operations, breaking 453 into 400 + 50 + 3. (This is exactly what students are doing in the usual method, but they do not always realise this.)

```
      638            638           638            638
    × 400           × 50          ×  3          × 453
    ------          -----         -----         ------
    255200    +     31900    +     1914    =    289014
```

Some students enjoy using **the box method** of working out long multiplication.

$$638 \times 453$$

- Break the numbers down into (600 + 30 + 8) × (400 + 50 + 3).
- Write them in the grid as indicated.
- Use your set square, or L shaped piece of card to identify where two numbers meet.
- First enter the zeros. Then multiply the two single figures. Then add the rows.

×	600	30	8	+
400	240000	12000	3200	255200
50	30000	1500	400	31900
3	1800	90	24	1914
	271800	13590	3624	Total: 289014

Reverse the L shaped card and use as a marker

- Add the sub-totals to get the total in the bottom right box. Then check by adding the columns to see if the answer is the same.

Tip

Some students find it difficult to break down the number by which they are multiplying. Example: 364 × 27

```
  3 6 4
×   2 7
-------
```

Break down the number by which you are multiplying into 7 and 20

```
    3 6 4
  ×   2 7
  -------
          7
         20
```

Move the zero to the left of the line so the ten is in place. Work out.

```
    3 6 4          3 6 4
  ×   2 7        ×   2 7
  -------        -------
          7        2 5 4 8 ‖ 7
  0 ‖ 2 0́        7 2 8 0 ‖ 2
                 -------
                 9 8 2 8
```

Putting the multiples in place beside the line can help a student see what he is doing.

Long division

What is the problem? Long division causes many students without specific mathematical weaknesses a problem. Weaker students often find it incomprehensible. They need to be able to work out times tables, recognise number relationships, subtract, deal with place value and understand the principle of the decimal place and they often find that the variety of elements causes overload.

Where to start: Again it is probably better to work to develop the technique that a student recognises, but also develop a *pattern* of working, through which a student actually moves physically.

First work out the times table of the divisor.

Once that is in place the student can use it without having to interrupt the flow of the physical patterning used to carry out the steps of the task

23
46
69
92
115
138
161
184
207
230

(Go up to 10×. It helps you be sure you are right.)

1. Use your thumb or a piece of paper to cover the numbers you are not using.

2. Say:
   '23 goes into 59 twice.
   2 × 23 = 46
   Take 46 from 59.'

3. Draw an **arrow** as you bring down the next number

4. Check table.
   '23 goes into 135 five times.
   5 × 23 = 115
   Take 115 from 135.'

5. Draw an arrow as you bring down the next number

6. '23 goes into 207 nine times.
   9 × 23 = 207
   There is nothing left over.'

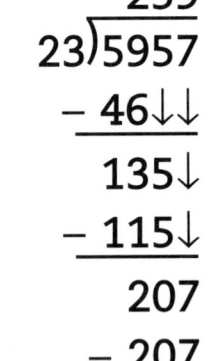

Do:

Encourage the student when doing long division to:

- **Talk** his way through the task.
- Use **movement** to learn what part of the pattern comes next.
- Include **arrows** and **subtraction signs** to see what to do.
- **Separate** the process of working out the table in order to ...
- **Simplify** the variety of tasks needing to be done together.

Using different senses will help a technique become automatic.

Key skills – addition and subtraction

As you write the sums out to work them out, place a mark at the bottom right to make sure that you start in the right place. Keep decimal points in line. Use estimation to think about the sort of answer you should expect and remember that in subtraction it is **BOTTOMS AWAY.**

Go through your paces to think through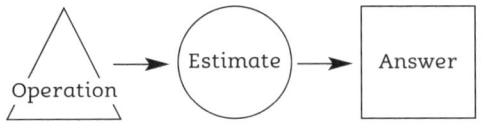

1. a) $\begin{array}{r} 345 \\ + 562 \leftarrow \\ \hline \end{array}$ b) $\begin{array}{r} 894 \\ + 937 \\ \hline \end{array}$ c) $\begin{array}{r} 9846 \\ + 1389 \\ \hline \end{array}$

2. There are 265 students in Year 9, 281 students in Year 10 and 304 students in Year 11. How many students are there altogether?

3. Alex buys three things at the supermarket. They cost £14.75, £18.36 and £2.27. What was the total cost?

4. a) $\begin{array}{r} 762 \\ -381 \leftarrow \\ \hline \end{array}$ b) $\begin{array}{r} 567 \\ -196 \\ \hline \end{array}$ c) $\begin{array}{r} 394 \\ -218 \\ \hline \end{array}$

5. There are 832 students in a school. On Monday 57 were absent. How many were present?

6. Sam has £25.00 in his wallet. He spends £4.99 on one item and £12.86 on another. How much money does he have left?

7. a) $\begin{array}{r} 245.92 \\ + 62.04 \\ \hline \end{array}$ b) $\begin{array}{r} 749.3520 \\ + 4.3643 \\ \hline \end{array}$ c) $\begin{array}{r} 204.02 \\ + 4501.50 \\ \hline \end{array}$

    d) $\begin{array}{r} 6040.52 \\ - 3928.25 \\ \hline \end{array}$ e) $\begin{array}{r} 200.75 \\ - 82.40 \\ \hline \end{array}$ f) $\begin{array}{r} 8359.67 \\ - 471.85 \\ \hline \end{array}$

8. Rearrange and work out
    a)   238 + 643   b)   402 + 659   c)   701.2 + 34

    d)   45.65 + 276.4   e)   304 + 1.625   f)   657.5 – 34.25

    g)   836.33 – 547.12   h)   2.25 – 0.125

Key skills – multiplication and division

*Remember to use your tables square. For long division, write out the table and use arrows to help you with the pattern. Don't forget to go through your **PACES** to think out:*

 Operation  Estimate  Answer

1. Rearrange to use the method of long multiplication that you prefer.

   a) 456 × 16   b) 734 × 27   c) 206 × 42

2. Polly organises a trip to a theme park. If 25 people are going and each of them pays her £19.75, how much money does she collect?

3. Tom orders boxes of sweets. Each box costs £11.95. He orders 48 boxes. How much will it cost?

4. Work out using long division:

   a) 437 ÷ 23   b) 1104 ÷ 23   c) 14352 ÷ 23

5. Nineteen postmen share a £555,845 win on the lottery. How much will each of them get?

6. All 14 members of a youth club save the same amount of money. If the total saved is £735, how much did each of them save?

7. Andy collects £15 each from the 38 people in his office. The money is then shared between 5 charities. How much will each charity get?

8. On a 14 day bicycling holiday, Steve and Paul want to travel 882 miles. How far should they travel each day?

2

Name: _____ Date: _____

TARGET

I can subtract large numbers accurately. I can subtract using the decimal point.

☐ ☐ ☐ ☐ ☐

4

Name: _____ Date: _____

TARGET

I am confident in the skills I need to use long division.

☐ ☐ ☐ ☐ ☐

1

Name: _____ Date: _____

TARGET

I can add large numbers accurately. I can add using the decimal point.

☐ ☐ ☐ ☐ ☐

3

Name: _____ Date: _____

TARGET

I am confident in the skills I need to use long multiplication.

☐ ☐ ☐ ☐ ☐

Simple percentages – finding 10% and 1%

What is the problem? A student who has grasped place value as a method of finding multiplying or dividing by 10 and 100 needs to realise that he can use this to find 10% and 1%.

Where to start: Once a student has developed an awareness of the size of numbers, he can see that moving a number across the decimal point makes it 10×, 100×, 1000× bigger or smaller. This knowledge can be transferred to find 10% of a number or 1% of a number. The slider used on page 50 can be used to illustrate this.

What is 10% of 375?

Where would the decimal point come in this whole number?

375.0

$\longrightarrow$

Move the whole number once to the right to make it 10 times smaller. The figure 5 will move across the decimal point.

37.5

What is 1% of 375?

Where would the decimal point come in this whole number?

375.0

$\longrightarrow \longrightarrow$

Move the number twice to the right. Two figures will move across the decimal point to make it 100 times smaller.

3.75

Other percentages

Where to next? The student can extend the ability to find 10% and 1% to obtain to find other percentages through doubling and halving without a calculator.

$$10\% + 10\% = 20\%$$
$$10\% + 20\% = 30\%$$
$$10\% \div 2 = 5\%$$
$$5\% \div 2 = 2\tfrac{1}{2}\%$$

By doubling or halving 10% , a student can work out most of the percentages he needs to be able to use.

VAT at 17½% is the most likely awkward percentage.

This is: 10% + 5% + 2½%

For example: The cost price for a hi-fi system is £250.00. The shop then adds VAT at 17½%. What price is the hi-fi in the shop?

- Move the number across the decimal point once to find 10% – so 250.00 becomes 25.00.
- Halve that to find 5%. Half of 25.00 is 12.50.
- Halve that to find 2½%. Half of 12.50 is 6.25
- Now add together 25.00 + 12.50 + 6.25 = 43.75

The VAT charged is £43.75.

Remember to check back to see that you have answered the question!

The question wants to know the **price in the shop**. That means add together the cost price and the VAT.

£250.00 + £43.75 = £293.75

Finding 10% and 1%

Think where the decimal point is in each of the numbers, then move the number across the decimal point to find 10% or 1%.

> **Remember**: *Move the number across the decimal point **once** to find 10% and twice to find 1%.*
>
> *£3482   10% of £3482 is £348.20   1% of £3482 is £34.82*

1. What is 10% of 180?

2. What is 10% of 375g?

3. What is 10% of 4525km?

4. What is 10% of £62.50?

5. A television costs £285. It is in the sale with a saving of 10%. How much will the sale price be?

6. A car's price is reduced by 10%. The original price was £8450. How much would I save?

7. What is 10% of 34.20?

8. What is 1% of 250?

9. There are 800 pupils in a school. 1% of the pupils go to Florida for their summer holiday. How many pupils go to Florida?

10. There are 1500 children born in one town in 1990. 10% of the children are left-handed. 1% of the children are left-handed and blue-eyed.

    a) How many children are left-handed?
    b) How many children are blue-eyed and left-handed?

Finding awkward percentages

Use doubling and halving to help you work out percentages of these numbers.

> **Remember**: Two lots of 10% make 20%. Half of 10% is 5%.
>
> Jane saved 35% on a £700 television. What did she pay?
>
> - Move the number across the decimal point to make it 10 times smaller.
> - 10% is £70. Three lots of 10% make 30%.
>   Three lots of £70 make £210.
> - 5% is half of 10%. Half of £70 is £35. Add it to 30%.
>   £210 + £35 = £245.
> - Jane saves £245. She **pays** £700 – £245 = £455.

1. What is 10% of 120? What is 20% of 120?

2. What is 10% of £46? What is 5% of £46?

3. What is 10% of $380? What is 15% of $380?

4. If 10% of a number is 26, what was the original number?

5. If 1% of a number is 26, what was the original number?

6. The cost price of a television set is £680. VAT is charged at $17\frac{1}{2}$%. What is the price of the television in the shop?

7. VAT at $17\frac{1}{2}$% is charged on DVDs. Before VAT is added the price of a DVD is £20. What will the final price be?

8. Mr. Smith bought his car for £8,750. He sold is after a year for 20% less than he paid. How much did he sell it for?

9. Terry bought his house for £120,000. He sold it for 15% more than he paid. What was the selling price of the house?

10. Ali's grandfather said he would give Ali 30% of anything he saved over one year. Ali saved £1 each week for 52 weeks. How much did his grandfather give him at the end of the year?

TARGET 1

Name: _____ Date: _____

I can use 10% and 1% of a number.

☐ ☐ ☐ ☐

TARGET 2

Name: _____ Date: _____

I can use 10% to help me find 5% and $2\frac{1}{2}$%. From that I can find $17\frac{1}{2}$%.

☐ ☐ ☐ ☐

TARGET 3

Name: _____ Date: _____

I can use 10% to find other percentages of a number.

☐ ☐ ☐ ☐

TARGET 4

Name: _____ Date: _____

I can understand questions that ask me to find out percentages and work out the answers.

☐ ☐ ☐ ☐

Using the Calculator

What is the problem? Calculators make maths easy, don't they? They stop students using real maths skills and make them depend on technology.

Is this true? Well – it could be, in some ways. **BUT** the main problem with this simplification is that if a student does not understand what he is doing, *he will not know whether the answer he gets is right or wrong*. Students who are insecure with maths and cannot estimate, generally accept whatever answer the calculator provides, *even if it is clearly impossible*.

Where to start: Students should be encouraged to use a calculator with a display that shows him which buttons he has pressed. He can then

- check the accuracy of the figures
- check the signs
- look to see if brackets are needed

This helps overcome the problem that *most mistakes with the calculator are caused by putting in the wrong information*.

Tip

Calculators: Use a **DAL** (Direct Algebraic Logic) calculator. It allows a student to enter the elements of an equation in the exact order they appear in the textbook. A two-line display enables a student to see the equation as well as the answer at the same time, which makes it easier to check that he has inputted the right numbers in the right order.

$$2\ 3 + (4\ 5 \div 9) =$$
$$28$$

For a student to know if the answer he is getting is likely to be correct, he needs to know roughly what the answer should be. And this takes him back to understanding of number and estimation.

Remember to be a STUD.

See : Talk : Understand : Do

Vocalisation can help with input. The student can say what he is doing as he is carrying out the task.

312.25 + 67.50

The student says aloud, 'Three hundred and twelve, (or three, one, two), point two five plus sixty seven, (or six, seven), point five equals'.

- Slowing down can help increase accuracy.
- Using a card or a set square to outline each figure as it is transferred to the calculator can help increase accuracy.
- Checking each copied number before moving to the next step can help increase accuracy.

Where to next: Simple functions – adding, subtracting, multiplying and dividing – can be improved with practice. The calculator can be invaluable for more complex tasks, such as indices, sine/cosine/tangents or working out fractions. Students can often carry out these tasks at the point where they are being taught, BUT they do not retain the skill.

As part of the note writing process, provide the student with sheets of little boxes – or get him to draw his own. Write **every stage** of the process down so that the student has a resource he can use to check how to carry out tasks. He can then use this whenever he needs it.

Posters displaying step-by-step instructions for carrying out different tasks on the calculator can be useful, as can laminated sheets to which a student can have easy access whenever needed.

Tip

Coloured revision cards can also be useful for helping students remember how to use their calculators to carry out tasks, such as adding fractions or implementing the sine rule.

Write out the what the sum is: $4\frac{3}{4} + \frac{5}{8} =$

Draw a series of small squares to represent calculator buttons and show the exact order in which the buttons must be pressed to work out the answer.

| 4 | $a^b/_c$ | 3 | $a^b/_c$ | 4 | + | 5 | $a^b/_c$ | 8 | = | 5 | $a^b/_c$ | 3 | $a^b/_c$ | 8 |

The student can now use the cards to check how to use his calculator.

If you want to get the most from your calculator, you need to know that

Calculators work out sums in a particular order.

- Brackets
- Other – such things as powers and square roots
- Division
- Multiplication
- Addition
- Subtraction

Activity

$30 + 5 \div 7 = 5$

Put it into your calculator exactly as it appears.
The answer it gives is 30.71428571.

What went wrong? The calculator did $5 \div 7$ first: then it added 30.

To make it do what you want, add brackets.
$(30 + 5) \div 7$

The calculator will do the bit in brackets first, then divide.
$(30 + 5) \div 7 = 5$

This is usually called **BODMAS** *for short.*

(If you like mnemonics, you could remember Brush Off Dog Mess And Soon.)

Using your calculator

Make sure you know the sequence of steps needed to carry out these tasks. Use estimation to think about the sort of answer you should expect.

First steps.

	Operation	Estimate	Answer

1   Add 399.5, 6021 and 85.22.

2   What is the difference between 28.75 and 5.04.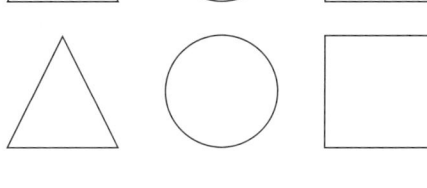

3   If 22 people each spend £29 at the shop, how much have they spent?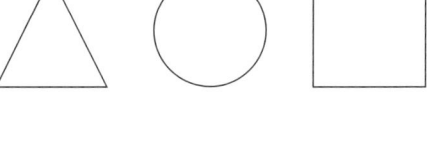

4   Nine people shared equally a win of £1 222 056 on the Lottery. How much did they get each?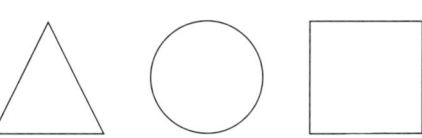

*Make sure you know **how** to do these tasks **before** trying them.*

Using the x² key and the √ key.

5   What is 5 squared?

6   What is the square of 13?

7   What is the square root of 400?

8   What is the square root of 1156?

Using the fraction key.

9   What is the total of $5\frac{1}{2} + 4\frac{2}{3}$

10 $15\frac{1}{3} - 8\frac{7}{8} =$

11 $4\frac{3}{8} \times 6\frac{2}{3} =$

12 $12\frac{1}{2} \div 4\frac{7}{8} =$

Using your calculator

Remember **BODMAS** *and use brackets to make you calculator carry out tasks in the right order. Use estimation to think about the sort of answer you should expect.*

1 $25 + 5 \div 10 - 6$

Use one set of brackets to make the answer to this sum come to

a) -3 b) 26.25 c) 19.5

2 $25 + 5 \div 10 - 6$

Use two sets of brackets to make the answer to this sum come to 7.5.

3 $\dfrac{37.5 + 292.3}{22.8 \times 4.9}$

a) Estimate the answer to this question. b) use a calculator to work out the answer. (Give the answer to 3 decimal places.)

Using the π key

(Advice: Put the formula into a triangle.
Use like number bond triangles.)

The area of a circle is worked out using the formula

πr^2 (r = radius)

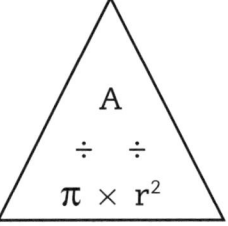

4   If the radius of a circle is 7 cm, what is its area?

5   If the radius of a circle is 12 m, what is its area?

The circumference of a circle is worked out using the formula **πd** (d is the diameter). Make a triangle like the one above.

6   If the diameter of a circle is 14.65 cm, what is the circumference?

7   If the diameter of a circle is 20 m, what is the circumference?

Name: _____ Date: _____

TARGET

I can use the square and square root keys with confidence.

☐ ☐ ☐ ☐ ☐

Name: _____ Date: _____

TARGET

I can use the π key on my calculator.

☐ ☐ ☐ ☐ ☐

Name: _____ Date: _____

TARGET

I can add, subtract, mulitply and divide accurately using my calculator.

☐ ☐ ☐ ☐ ☐

Name: _____ Date: _____

TARGET

I am confident that I can use the fraction key on my calculator.

☐ ☐ ☐ ☐ ☐

Target Maths – Skills Area 2: Acquiring Skills

81

Money

What is the problem?

Problems	Helpful points
Pounds and pence are different units – a student may find it difficult to convert.	Do more work on place value and the student will find money easier to understand.
Money **never** uses more than two decimal places.	Converting pence into pounds using coins can help make the process clear.
Large numbers can be confusing.	Rounding off and estimating can help understand answers.
Most questions that involve money are testing other skills as well.	Work on the basis that money means something to all students.

Where to start: For older students, money is the way into understanding many calculations. It motivates them! **Many students who protest that they have little understanding of maths, have a good grasp of the value of money.** Whereas sweets are often a good way to get a younger child to picture mathematical calculations, with older students, money works far better. They can teach themselves to think of whole number calculations as being money sums. Money also uses decimal places and can help a student extend understanding to numbers smaller than one whole one.

- Students can use a calculator to work out money – but they are often confused to find that a zero in the hundredths column is not shown. Remind them frequently. Get them to make a note of it in their glossaries, (see page 15).

£0.99

The skill developed in adding and subtracting 9 can be used to add on sums of money ending in 99p.

Add on a whole number of pounds and then **take off** one penny.

£3.20 + £1.99 would be £3.20 + £2.00 = £5.20 – 1p = £5.19

To take off an amount ending in 99p, **subtract** the whole number and **add** 1p.

A student who can understand calculations with money can work with decimals.

Working with money

*Think about whether the **units** are the same. Use estimation to think about the sort of answer you should expect.*

1 Mary went to the supermarket.

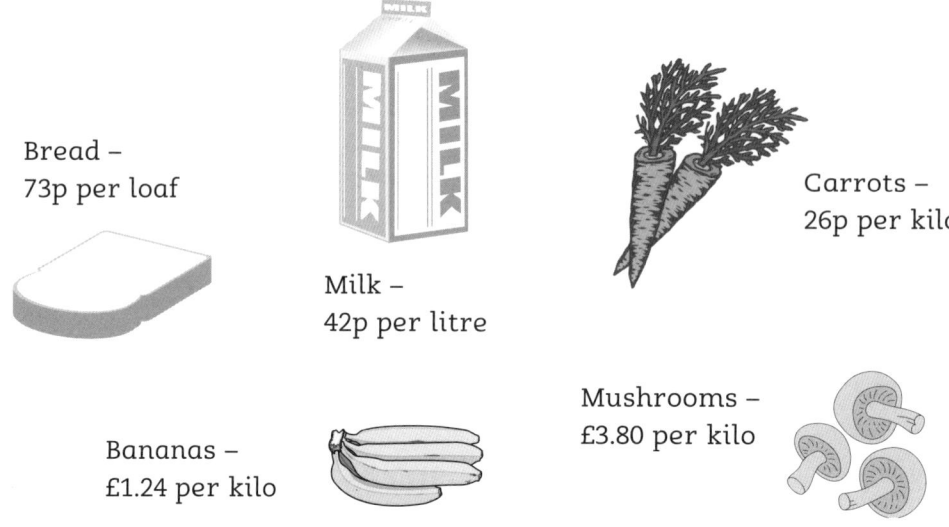

Bread – 73p per loaf

Milk – 42p per litre

Carrots – 26p per kilo

Mushrooms – £3.80 per kilo

Bananas – £1.24 per kilo

She had a £20 note. She bought

two loaves of bread,
four litres of milk,
half a kilo of carrots,
one and a half kilos of bananas and
250 grams of mushrooms.

How much change did she have after buying these items?

2 Mrs. Jones is taking her class to the zoo. Each of them has to pay £15.50 for the trip. If there are 23 people in the class, what is the total collected by Mrs. Jones?

If the total paid for entrance to the zoo is £207, and the remainder is the cost of the coach, how much is charged for the coach?

3 Seven people share a prize of £149 254.98. How much does each receive?

Working with money

*Think about whether the **units** are the same. Use estimation to think about the sort of answer you should expect.*

1 What is the total amount in Emma's money box if she has -

Value of coin	Number of coins	Value × Number of coins	Total value for each coin
£2	3	£2 × 3	£6
£1	7		
50p	13		
20p	52		
10p	26		
5p	44		
2p	124		
1p	68		
		Total	

2 Robert's car takes 48 litres of petrol. Petrol costs 83.5 pence per litre. How much in pence will it cost to fill up Robert's car?

How much is that in pounds and pence?

If Robert only has £30.00, what is the largest number of whole litres he can buy?

3 Pat is buying boxes of crisps for his shop. Each box contains 48 packets of crisps. If each packet of crisps costs 26 pence, how much will a box of crisps cost?

If Pat sells each packet of crisps for 35p, how much will he get for the whole box?

2

Name: ─────── Date: ───────

TARGET

I recognise when a question wants me to convert pence to pounds and pounds to pence.

☐ ☐ ☐ ☐

4

Name: ─────── Date: ───────

TARGET

I can deal with money sums that use both large and small quantities.

☐ ☐ ☐ ☐

1

Name: ─────── Date: ───────

TARGET

I can convert pence to pounds and pounds to pence.

☐ ☐ ☐ ☐

3

Name: ─────── Date: ───────

TARGET

I am confident that I can add, subtract, multiply and divide money.

☐ ☐ ☐ ☐

Measurements

What is the problem? A student who has grasped the meanings of prefixes will have some idea of the stages through which milli- leads to kilo-, but many of them are still confused between metric and imperial units of measurement. Ask any student how much he weighs and the chances are he will tell you in stones. Ask him how tall he is and he will know in feet and inches. He will talk about long distances in miles, and yet the majority of the work he has done on the subject in school will involve metric measurements.

Where to start: Students need a point of reference, so they can visualise how big a measurement is.

Conversion tables are all very well – and it would benefit most students to create a memory card to keep handy, but he needs to be able to say to himself '30 cm – that's a long ruler', or '2 m – that's how tall Uncle Bob is', or '1 km – that's from my house to the newsagents'.

A good point of reference is . . . . himself.

For example:

> 'I am **1 m 50 cm**, which is roughly **5 ft**,
> (which is the same as **60 inches**).'
> 'I weigh **48 kg**, which is roughly 7½ stone,
> (which is the same as **105 pounds**).'
> 'I live **8 km** from school,
> which is roughly the same as **5 miles**.'

From these points of certainty, he can decide on the **likelihood** of his answers. Estimation again comes into its own.

Conversion requires a student to turn one thing into another. There are only two ways to do it – to divide one measurement by the conversion factor or to multiply it.

1 inch ≈ 2.5 centimetres

(mental note: an inch is bigger than a centimetre)

[Remember the symbol ≈ Check you have written it down. ≈ *means* is the same as]

Karen's book is 15 inches long and 9 inches wide. What are these measurements in centimetres?

To convert, Karen must either multiply or divide.

15 × 2.5 = 37.5 cm   **or**   15 ÷ 2.5 = 6 cm

(Think: if an inch is bigger than a centimetre, it will take more centimetres to measure the same amount. Check this fact against your ruler.)

So 15 inches ≈ 37.5 centimetres and 9 inches ≈ 22.5 centimetres.

Visualisation can help a student see which process is right.

Using and converting measurements 1

Make a card that states how metric units relate with each other. On the other side make a similar chart of imperial measurements.

1 Complete this chart.

Imperial measures

12 inches	=	.... foot
.... feet	=	1 yard
.... yards	=	1 mile
.... fluid ounces	=	1 pint
.... pints	=	1 gallon
16 ounces (oz)	=	.... pound (lb)
.... pounds	=	1 stone
.... stones	=	1 ....
.... hundredweights	=	1 ....

2 How many inches are there in three feet?

3 How many pounds make half a stone?

Cont'd

4 Complete this chart.

Metric measures		
10 millimetres	=	1 ....
100	=	1 metre
.... millimetres	=	1 metre
.... metres	=	1 kilometre
100 centilitres	=	1 ....
1000 millilitres	=	1 ....
1000	=	1 gram
1000	=	1 kilogram
1000	=	1 tonne

5 How many metres are there in 5 kilometres?

6 How many grams are there in 1 tonne?

Using and converting measurements 2

Make a card that tells you the approximate conversion of metric and imperial measures.

1 Complete this chart of approximate conversions.

Imperial		Metric
1 inch	≈	......centimetres
1	≈	30 centimetres
5 miles	≈	8 ....
1 mile	≈	1.6 ....
1.75 pints	?	1 ....
1	≈	4.5 litres
2.2 pounds	≈	1 ....

2 How many ounces are there in five stone?

3 How many yards are there in 3 miles?

4 How many centimetres are roughly the same as 10 inches?

5 How many inches are there in 270 centimetres?

6 What would 7 gallons be in litres?

7 A baby weighs 17.6 pounds. What is that in kilograms?

8 Martin is 157 centimetres tall. How tall is he in inches? (to the nearest inch.)

9 A shop has 540 gallons of milk delivered. How much is that in litres?

10 Sue has to drive 85 miles to a meeting. How far is that in kilometres?

2

Name: _____ Date: _____

TARGET

I can recognise and use metric and imperial units of measurement.

☐ ☐ ☐ ☐

4

Name: _____ Date: _____

TARGET

I can use conversion factors to deal with other types of question.

☐ ☐ ☐ ☐

1

Name: _____ Date: _____

TARGET

I know how units of measurement relate to one another.

☐ ☐ ☐ ☐

3

Name: _____ Date: _____

TARGET

I can convert metric and imperial measurements when I am given the conversion factor.

☐ ☐ ☐ ☐

Time – Helping Students to Develop Time Skills

Many students experience difficulty with the concept of time. They have no understanding of the passage of time and cannot estimate time intervals. In addition they have no time skills and therefore cannot access the school curriculum. In this section we suggest strategies to improve time skills and in Skills Area 3 we will revisit time and develop strategies to access 'time' based problems in the curriculum.

What is the problem?

Most students will have started telling the time using an 'analogue' approach, may have picked up the 'digital' approach because they own a digital watch and may have never really mastered the 24 hour approach.

Where to start?

- The starting point is the 24 hour clock.
- Time should be introduced as a measurement skill.
- The students need to know the units of measure.

> 60 minutes = 1 hour
>
> 24 hours = 1 day

What measuring tool to use?

The most appropriate tool is a number line. Firstly, because they will have already used this. Secondly, it is a way of linking the three time systems and lastly it forms the basis for approaching time based problems in the curriculum. This tool will now be referred to as a 'time line', (*see resource sheet 5b*). It will help to resolve confusion and will add to the student's set of strategies to approach maths problems.

Introducing the 'time line'

The student needs to be given a few basic facts:

> - the new day starts at midnight
> - 12 noon is the midpoint of the day
> - 24 hour time is written with 4 numbers
> - the gap between one hour and the next is 60 minutes.

The student is now ready to mark his time line and start to use it. In an ideal situation he should make his own but time in senior schools rarely allows for this. Give the student a blank time line as in the *photocopiable sheet 5b or 5c*. To help him to become familiar with time lines ask him to mark the hours. The scale should be pointed out to the student, 6 sections between each hour.

Next the student needs to be helped to use a time to work out a problem. This is a shared activity. As the students move through the stages he needs to be shown how to mark his time line and make his calculations.

Stage 1 Whole hour to whole hour. You go on a school trip that starts at 1100 and finishes at 1400. How long did it take?

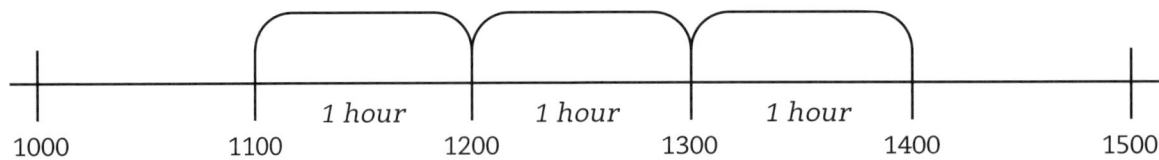

Answer =

Stage 2 Whole hour to beyond the next hour. You go on a school trip that start at 1000 and finishes at 1435. How long did it take?

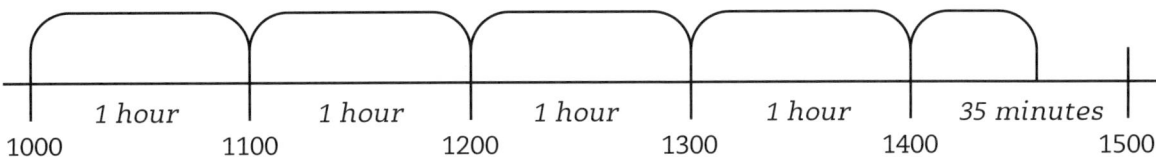

1 hour   1 hour   1 hour   1 hour   35 minutes

1000   1100   1200   1300   1400   1500

Answer =

Stage 3 Middle of first hour and beyond several hours.
You go on school trip that starts at 1015 and ends at 1445.

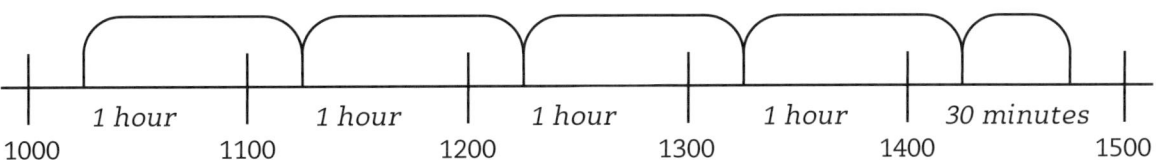

1 hour   1 hour   1 hour   1 hour   30 minutes

1000   1100   1200   1300   1400   1500

Answer =

Once the student has stepped through this sequence he needs to start using a time line working independently. He needs to start with the simple and move to the complex. The suggested sequence is set out on page 97.

- Start with movements along the line that involve whole hours. *Box 1*
- Next movements begin on the hour and not reach the next hour. *Box 2*
- Next movements go beyond the next hour. *Box 3*
- Next movements start in the middle of one hour and go beyond the next. *Box 4*
- Next movements go beyond several hours *Box 5*.

Ask the student to complete photocopiable sheet 2.15, page 97.

The next step is to move the student to a situation that he would meet within the class, for homework or in an exam. Give him a problem, a blank piece of paper and ask him to make his calculation. He needs to be able to quickly draw a time line, mark it simply and use it to make his calculation. Give him guidance on how to draw a quick time line.

How long is it from 9.45 to 1.15?

- *Use your rule draw a straight line.*
- *Mark six hours allowing two centimetres for each hour.*
- *Mark the halfway point of each hour.*

Now use this time line to solve the problem!

His sketch should look something like this:

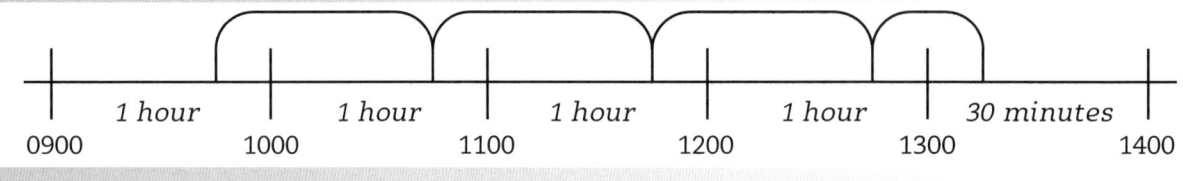

Lastly to extend the student's knowledge he needs to link the three time systems together. If time permits the student can make a time line linking 24 hour, digital and analogue if not he can be given a *photocopiable resource sheet 5a*.

Finding the time

Box 1

a) You go on a school trip. The bus leaves at 0900 and arrives at 1100. How long was the journey?

b) You go to a movie. It starts at 1900 and ends at 2100. How long did it last?

c) You go on a ferry to France. It leaves at 0700 and arrives at 1300. How long did it take?

Box 2

a) Your art lesson begins at 1100 and ends at 1155. How long did it last?

b) Your TV programme starts at 1900 and ends at 1940. How long did it last?

c) Your swimming lesson starts at 1400 and ends at 1445. How long did it last?

Box 3

a) The movie you watch starts at 1900 and ends at 2020. How long did it last?

b) Your football match started at 1600 and ended at 1730. How long did it last?

c) You go out at 1700 and come home at 1845. How long were you out?

Box 4

a) Your TV programme starts at 1635 and ends at 1705. How long did it last?

b) You start your computer game at 0915 and finish at 1020. How long did you play?

c) You go into a café at 1250 and come out at 1335. How long were you in the café?

Box 5

a) You go out to play a match at 1345 and come back at 1545. How long were you out?

b) The party starts at 1940 and ends at 2110. How long did it last?

c) Your exam starts at 0900 and ends at 1045. How long did it last?

Name: _____ Date: _____

TARGET 2

I can read an analogue clock and relate the times to a digital clock.

☐ ☐ ☐ ☐

Name: _____ Date: _____

TARGET 4

I can work out the passage of time using hours and minutes.

☐ ☐ ☐ ☐

Name: _____ Date: _____

TARGET 1

I can read a digital clock and relate times to my own day.

☐ ☐ ☐

Name: _____ Date: _____

TARGET 3

I can work out the passage of time using whole hours.

☐ ☐ ☐ ☐

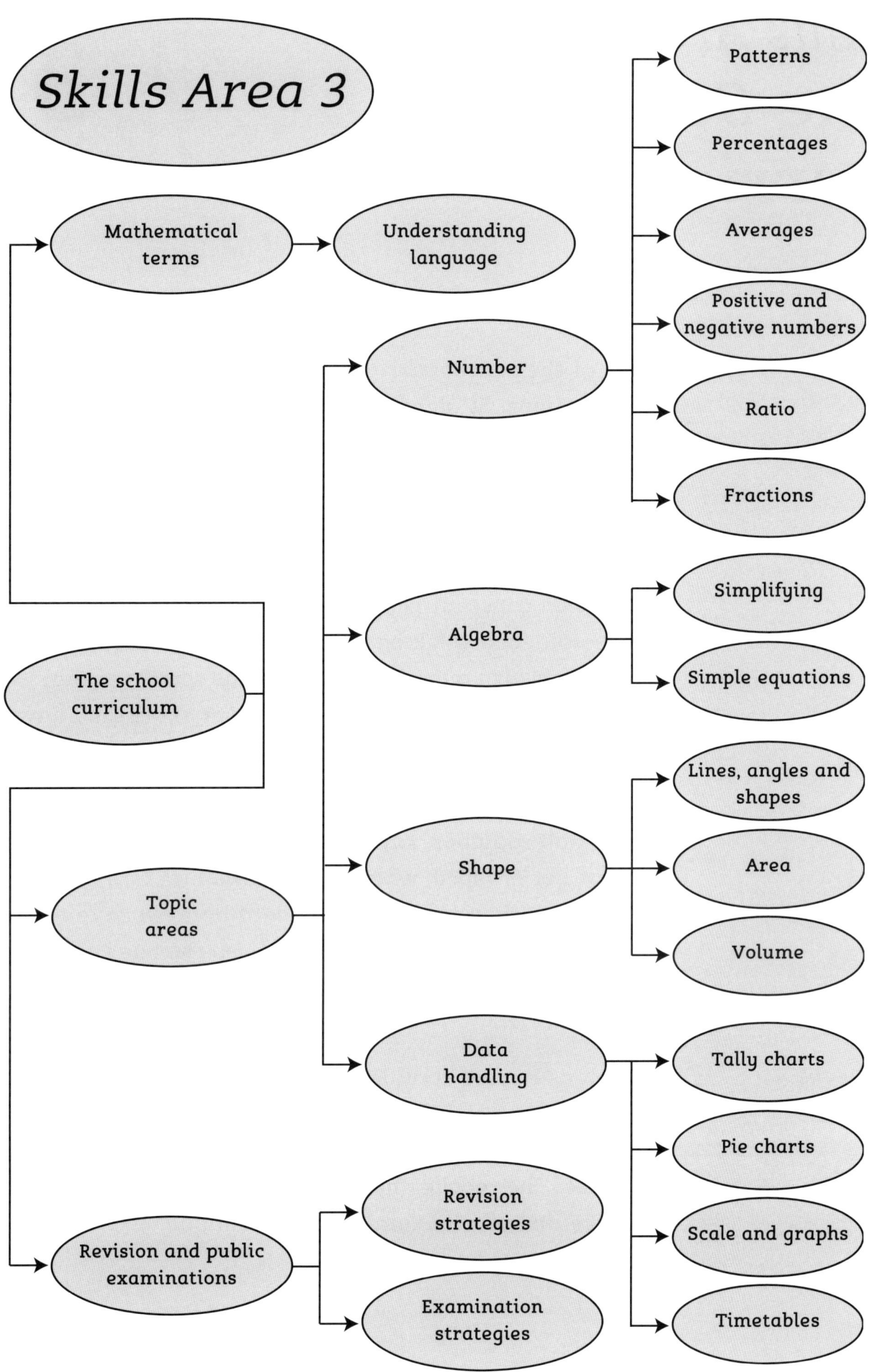

Skills Area 3

Mathematical terms → Understanding language

The school curriculum

Topic areas

Number → Patterns, Percentages, Averages, Positive and negative numbers, Ratio, Fractions

Algebra → Simplifying, Simple equations

Shape → Lines, angles and shapes, Area, Volume

Data handling → Tally charts, Pie charts, Scale and graphs, Timetables

Revision and public examinations → Revision strategies, Examination strategies

Skills Area 3
The School Curriculum

Much of the school curriculum involves working towards examinations. Students are expected to work at the pace dictated by the syllabus, which frequently means that, **just as they are beginning to get the hang of a topic, they are moved on to something new**.

Students who have difficulty absorbing and applying new ideas need constant **repetition**. They would benefit from one lesson each week being used to carry out practice of straightforward questions on previous topics, so that they are not given the chance to forget skills they have worked hard to acquire.

Homework, too, is more effective if it practises skills a student already has, rather than applying new ideas he has not yet grasped, when all it shows him is what he cannot do. Wherever possible, adapt homework to the level at which a student is working, so that he can be successful. This will have a direct effect on his behaviour in maths lessons.

As well as having confidence in working with number, algebra, shape and data handling, a student needs to be able to read and interpret questions and understand how to revise. The teacher must **reinforce** skills with regular practice and teach examination technique.

Mathematical Terms and Language

What is the problem? The words on page 103 have been selected from maths revision books – a student needs to learn, understand and remember a lot of terms that vary in difficulty. This makes a huge demand on a student's memory.

Take **obtuse**: *Are you being deliberately obtuse here?* Talking about maths? No. **Range**: *Cowboys ride on the open range.* Anything to do with the difference between the biggest and the smallest? No. **Acute**: *She had acute appendicitis.* Less than 90°, was it? No. **Volume**: *Turn down the volume on the radio and get me that volume of poetry.* Is that related to the capacity of a three-dimensional shape? No.

Mathematical (and scientific) words often have uses in everyday speech that makes their subject specific meaning confusing and hard to remember. Other words are used so infrequently that they are hard to retain.

However, if a student does not retain the specialist vocabulary and make connections between the words, he will find it impossible to interpret questions.

Where to start: Use the vocabulary regularly and ask the student to give the definition, use the term to describe what is happening or ask him to say the word that matches your description. Choose **Words of the Week** that are used, defined and tested. Use questions with missing words, so the student can provide the relevant term. Put up posters that use mathematical words – and change them regularly according to the topic. (*Remember: anything that stays up too long becomes wallpaper and students pay no attention to it.*) Specialist maths computer games can encourage students to recognise and use mathematical language.

And make sure that the student is adding to and maintaining his glossary of words (page 15).

A student who is successful in Skill Area 1 (Understanding of Number) should be able to unravel the language, break down problems and work out what he is being asked to do. Again, it requires constant practice if he is to transfer the techniques to long-term memory.

Maths is a Code

Remember that there is more to understanding maths than knowing what the words mean. Mathematicians use symbols – they are scattered all over the tasks a student is asked to decode. Some of them students do understand and sometimes they are simpler than the language. Other symbols need to be checked on regularly. They vary from simple lines to Greek letters and their purpose is to act as shorthand.

But shorthand is only useful if you can read it.

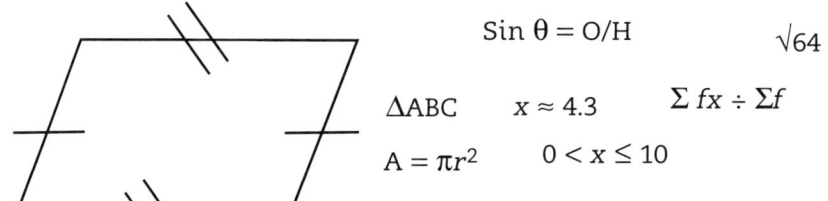

$\sin \theta = O/H$

$\sqrt{64}$

$\triangle ABC$ $\quad x \approx 4.3$ $\quad \Sigma fx \div \Sigma f$

$A = \pi r^2$ $\quad 0 < x \leq 10$

Remember: symbols are also part of this language of maths.

Mathematical terms

Where to next: Students should make their own glossaries that explain terms in words they can understand, with examples they can use to help them remember (see page 15).

Some words students need to understand

cube	square number	factor
square root	prime number	cube root
multiple	integer	prime factor
significant figure	decimal place	indices
equivalent fraction	percentage	ratio
substition	simplifing	expanding
factorising	expression	formula
simultaneous equations	right angle	obtuse angle
reflex angle	acute angle	complementary angle
supplementary angle	perpendicular	vertical
horizontal	parallel	equilateral
scalene	isosceles	square
rhombus	polygon	parallelogram
rectangle	trapezium	kite
hemisphere	solid	face
edge	vertex	cube
cuboid	prism	cylinder
sphere	area	perimeter
pyramid	net	bisector
bearings	conversion factors	locus
symmetry	line symmetry	plane of symmetry
rotational symmetry	transformations	reflection
rotation	enlargement	translation
congruent/congruence	similar/similarity	hypotenuse
correlation	circumference	volume
line of best fit	probability	tally chart
frequency	pictograms	bar charts
stem and leaf diagrams	line graphs	frequency polygons
pie charts	average	range
mean	median	mode
mid-interval values	cumulative frequency	interquartile range
box and whisker plots		

So many different words can easily be intimidating!

Memory techniques

- Link vocabulary with *pictures*. If trying to remember a **plane of symmetry**, take a drawing of an aeroplane and put in the plane of symmetry.

- Use *colour* to make connections. Put information about circles on coloured circles - so that when recalling the circle facts, they are red, whereas facts about rectangles are blue.

- Join vocabulary to an illustration that can help tie together the word and the meaning.

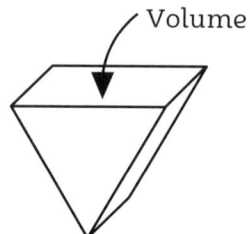

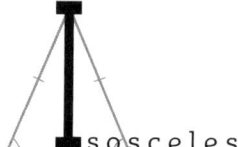

Tip
Remembering formulae

Try associating **colour** with particular rules.

For example: you want to remember the formula for the circumference of a circle.

Draw a circle

Around the edge of the circle write the formula in words **and** using letters.

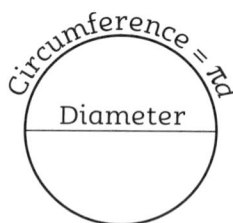

Circumference = π × diameter

$$C = \pi d$$

Now when you want to remember how to work out the circumference of a circle, close your eyes and picture the coloured image with the words on it. *Visualise.*

Understanding questions

You do not have to work out the answers to these questions. **Highlight** *the key words and think about what you are being asked to do and look up any vocabulary you cannot remember.* **Put any missing words into your glossary**. *(The answers are provided if you want to work them out.)*

[1] Simplify: a) $c^3 \times c^3$ b) $3n + 6p - 2p + 3n - n$

[2] Solve the equations: a) $4t + 6 = 3t + 11$ b) $3(2d - 5) = 9$

[3]

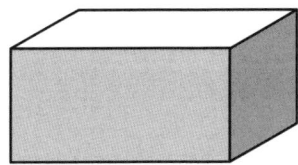

Calculate the volume of a cuboid that is 4.5 m long, 2 m wide and 3 m high.

[4]

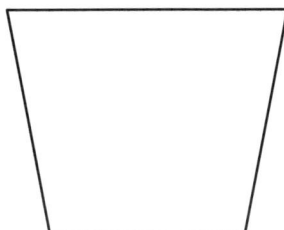

Mike wants to use these tiles in his kitchen. Draw some ways in which the tiles could tessellate. Draw six additional tiles.

[5] Four friends, Ali, Ben, Carol and Diane win £8000. They share it in the ratio 2 : 1 : 3 : 4. How much will Carol get?

[6] Martin organises a discount of ⅜ on the price of a trampoline for a children's club.

What is ⅜ written as: a) a decimal?   b) a percentage?

c) The normal price of a trampoline is £560. Work out what the children's club will have to pay.

Understanding questions

You do not have to work out the answers to these questions. Highlight the key words and think about what you are being asked to do and look up any vocabulary you cannot remember. **Put any missing words into your glossary.** *(The answers are provided if you want to work them out.)*

1 Calculate the angle AOB.

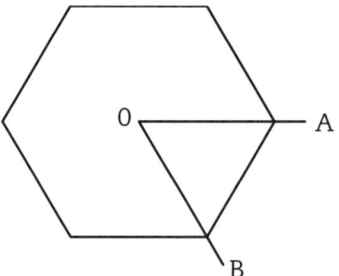

2 Expand and simplify: $2b(b - 5) + b(b + 2)$

3 In triangle ABC, the lines AB and BC are equal. Angle BAC is 50.

What is the name for this type of triangle?

Calculate the value of angle ACB.

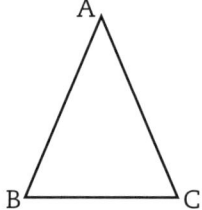

4 A bag contains 5 blue counters, 7 red counters, 2 green counters and 6 yellow counters.

Kate picks out one counter without looking. What is the probability that the counter is blue?

What is the probability that the counter is not green?

5 Sadie measures the length of 20 leaves. Their lengths (to the nearest centimetre) are:

1	3	2	4	1
2	3	3	2	5
3	2	3	4	1
3	2	1	5	3

What length is a) the median, b) the mode, c) the mean?

TARGET 2

Name: _____ Date: _____

I understand these mathematical symbols and have recorded them in my glossary.

☐ ☐ ☐ ☐

TARGET 4

Name: _____ Date: _____

I go through my PACES before I start to answer the question.

☐ ☐ ☐ ☐

TARGET 1

Name: _____ Date: _____

I have regularly added new words to my mathematical glossary.

☐ ☐ ☐ ☐

TARGET 3

Name: _____ Date: _____

I read questions three times before I start work and highlight key words and figures.

☐ ☐ ☐ ☐

Number

What is the problem? By the time students are in secondary education, they are very familiar with working with number. They are also often very familiar with failing to do so successfully. This expectation of failure will contaminate every newly introduced topic and understanding can falter when answers are worked out incorrectly due to poor grasp of number.

Where to start:

Do:

- **Reinforce core skills continually.** You cannot count on the fact that a process understood and used one day will also be understood and used successfully the next.

- **Give credit for what is done correctly.** Let the student know what he is doing right and celebrate his success. Then give him a tip towards making more progress. If he is using the right method, but getting his tables wrong, tell him so. He can then use a strategy, like a tables square, to attack the part of the process that is the problem, while knowing that he is getting the rest of the task right. This will increase, rather than shatter, confidence.

- **Not all students do things in the way you have taught them.** If the method is a variation on the one taught, get the student to explain to you what he is doing – he has often developed a successful strategy that works for him, and cannot comprehend why you are asking him to change.

- **Make use of peer mentoring.** If a student is not responding to your explanation, try getting him to work with a friend who is carrying out the task successfully. It will help both partners to develop understanding.

- **Use tools students already understand.** Hundred squares, table squares, number lines all make it easier for a student to extend his skills into other areas.

If a student has developed his confidence with number through working on the skills in areas 1 (Understanding of Number) and 2 (Acquiring Skills), he will have strategies at his fingertips to help him with basic number work. He will be able to use these to support more advanced work.

A wall of number

Mathematical understanding depends on knowing what was done before. Constant repetition and reinforcement of the basics is needed to make sure that students can carry out tasks.

Use a wall to show **small, achievable targets** that build on previous knowledge. Have the student shade in each area as he becomes confident in dealing with it. As the number of shaded areas increase, he will be able to see that his skills are developing.

Squares Cubes Roots	Standard form	Triangle numbers Fibonacci sequences	Value for money	Ratio
Prime number Multiple Factor	Sequences	Percentage profit Percentage loss	Mean Median Mode	
Mental maths	Number patterns	Tables	Percentages	Averages
Addition	Subtraction	Multiplication	Division	

The skills on the wall can be broken down into small steps, so that the student can see that he is making progress.

Addition, for example, could be taken apart to read:

Number bonds within 10		Adding on 11		Using a hundred square to add	
Counting in fives	Counting on from any point on a line		Counting in twos		Adding on 9
Recognise symbol		Counting in ones		Recognise language	

Other bricks could be added to extend learning. (Note: walls start at the *bottom* and **build** on understanding.)

Number patterns

Where to next: A student who has grasped Skills Areas 1 (Understanding of Number) and 2 (Acquiring Skills) will have an awareness of number and the ways in which different number patterns work. He may well, however, need to have his memory of them refreshed regularly.

The **Hundred Square** is a good resource for getting a student to mark in a variety of patterns and can be made a quick five minute practice task. It can be used for

- Marking in different **times tables**
- Identifying **multiples** of a number (multiples of 3: 6, 9, 24, 60)
- Identifying **factors** of a number (factors of 12: 1, 2, 3, 4, 6, 12)
- Marking in **prime numbers** (numbers divisible by themselves and 1 only)
- Marking in **square numbers** ($2^2 = 4$, $3^2 = 9$, $4^2 = 16$, etc.)
- Marking in **square roots** ($\sqrt{4} = 2$, $\sqrt{9} = 3$, $\sqrt{16} = 4$, etc.)

- Marking in **cube numbers and cube roots**. (True it only works for numbers from 1 – 4, but most students will probably only need to remember the addition of $5^3 = 125$ and $10^3 = 1000$.)
- Marking in **triangle numbers** (1, 3, 6, 10, 15, 21, etc.)
- Identifying numbers in the **Fibonacci sequence** (obtained by adding the two previous answers, e.g. 0, 1, 1, 2, 3, 5, 8, 13, 21, 34)

Some of these number patterns will be used far more frequently than others, but a student will benefit from building up a confident recognition of all these terms.

Tip

Once students have begun to build up a level of confidence in recognising the different types of number pattern

provide them with a booklet of hundred squares

Ensure they always give each page a heading and as they complete the practice squares, they will build up a visual resource bank of the variety of patterns involved in highlighting the correct squares.

Repetition builds memory

Percentages

What is the problem? Students have to carry out a sequence of tasks, in order, dealing with larger numbers often including decimal places.

Where to start: Students who have worked on Skills Area 2 (Acquiring Skills) should be able to find 1% or 10% of a number and use doubling and halving to discover other percentages. To many of them, this is the easiest and most logical way to work with percentages and they find it difficult to retain methods that require them to carry out a mathematical operation.

However, in order to progress towards higher level skills, a student will need to become more familiar with other possibilities.

Where to next: To find percentages, it can help a student to vocalise the task as he is doing it. As he says '**per cent**', teach him to draw the required number over 100: as he says '**of**', teach him to draw a multiplication sign, so that as he says

$$\text{"25\% of £40"}$$

he will automatically write

$$\frac{25}{100} \times 40 =$$

The positioning of the **40** indicates that the student can cancel down the numbers (if he is working without a calculator), saying '10 goes into 40 four times. 10 goes into 100 ten times'. Once the task has been written as a calculation, it becomes easier to complete, becoming

$$\frac{25}{10} \times 4 =$$

If he looks again he can see that he can cancel further.

Again linking motor memory, visual memory and auditory memory to a task means a student uses three of his senses to carry it out and makes it more likely that it transfers to long term memory.

Percentage profit and percentage loss

Making up something to jog the memory can be a useful tool to help a student carry out a task. This can include learning a formula, an image, a story, a rhyme – or, indeed, anything that proves memorable to an individual. The formula

$$\frac{\text{change}}{\text{original}} \times 100 = \text{percentage change}$$

can be remembered by itself – or you can make up something silly like:

coot loo = Change Over Original Times 100

The brain remembers the ridiculous best!

Finding the original price

This is probably the most difficult idea for students with a weakness in mathematics.

Although house prices are not very interesting, they do appear on examination questions quite often!

Lee is selling his house for £280 000. This is 40% more than he paid for it five years ago. How much did he pay for his house?

Possibly the easiest way for a student to **see** how to answer a question like this is to draw a line.

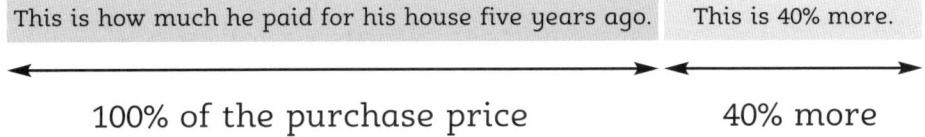

This is how much he paid for his house five years ago.   This is 40% more.

100% of the purchase price   40% more

So £280 000 is 100% + 40% or 140% of the original purchase price of the house.

Find 1% of the original price and multiply by 100

$$\frac{280\,000}{140} \times 100 = 200\,000$$

The price Lee paid for his house was £200 000

(If the student reverses the 140 and the 100, the answer will be bigger than the new higher price, and therefore, common sense should tell him that the answer is wrong.)

Always encourage students to use estimation and common sense to test if answers are likely.

113

Finding percentages

You can use your calculator to help you. *Remember to say out loud what you are doing as you write down the figures. You can use a mnemonic to help you recall how to work out percentage profit or percentage loss.*

example

Work out 15% of £525. $\frac{15}{100} \times 525 = £78.75$

(Percentage profit or loss: remember coot loo) If Ben buys a car for £2500 and sells it for £750, what is his percentage loss? (Change over Original times 100)

$\frac{1750}{2500} \times 100 = 70.$ His percentage loss is 70%.

1 Work out

a) 10% of 89   b) 22% of 550   c) 35% of 280   d) 14% of 882

2 Clare got 9 out of 10 for her maths test. What is that expressed as a percentage?

3 She got 18 out of 20 for her science test. What is that as a percentage?

4 Three other people taking the same science test got 19, 13 and 15. Change their marks into percentages.

5 Mr. Smith bought a painting at a car boot sale for £50.00. He sold it later for £350. What was his percentage profit?

6 Anna bought her first car for £1200. She sold it later for £840. What was her percentage loss?

7 Mr. Smith has just sold a table for £675. He made a 35% profit. For what price did he buy the table? (Check how to find the *original price*.)

8 Ben has just sold his motorbike for £480. This is 20% less than he paid for it. What was the price he paid?

2

Name: _____ Date: _____

TARGET

I can express one number out of another as a percentage.

□ □ □ □

4

Name: _____ Date: _____

TARGET

I can find the original price when I am given the new price and the percentage change.

□ □ □ □

1

Name: _____ Date: _____

TARGET

I can find a percentage of a number.

□ □ □ □

3

Name: _____ Date: _____

TARGET

I can work out percentage profit or percentage loss.

□ □ □ □

Averages

What is the problem? A student's first difficulty is remembering the meaning of **mean, median, mode** and **range**. The second is sorting through lists of numbers. This can be a major problem for a student with difficulty in short-term memory for number, who can reverse numbers and frequently fails to copy correctly.

Where to start: Improve accuracy by teaching a student to:

- Cover most of the numbers so that he can focus on them one or two at a time. (Or use a set square as shown on page 24.)
- Work down a column rather than across a row, as the columns are often shorter and easier to follow.
- Use different coloured highlighters to identify numbers from the same group.

Mode: one meaning of mode is **fashion (à la mode)**. If you are looking for the mode of a distribution, you are looking for the most fashionable and popular number.

1	3	5	2	4	1	1
2	3	6	2	5	2	1
2	4	6	2	3	2	2

The number 2 appears eight times, which is more than any other, so it is the **mode**.

If two or more numbers appear the same number of times, they are both the **mode**.

Median: the **middle** number or **medium** one of the group.

Rearrange the group in order to find which one comes in the middle. At the simplest level – take a long strip of squared paper, write the first number in the first square and so on across the strip, then cut or tear the strip off after the final number and fold it in half, and the student will see which number is in the middle. If there are an odd number of values, the answer will be a single number. If there are an even number of values, it will be halfway between two numbers.

↓

1 1 1 1 2 2 2 2 2 2 2 2 3 3 3 4 4 5 5 6 6

Mean: add all the values together and then divide by the number of values.

$$\frac{1 + 1 + 1 + 1 + 2 + 2 + 2 + 2 + 2 + 2 + 2 + 2 + 3 + 3 + 3 + 4 + 4 + 5 + 5 + 6 + 6}{21}$$

Answer: 2.81 (to 2 dp)

Range: the biggest value take away the smallest value.

6 – 1 = 5

Finding the average

*Use a ruler, set square or piece of paper to help you concentrate on one row or column at a time. Make a tally chart to record **each number in order**. You can use colour to help you see which numbers belong together.*

example

1 4 5 2 5 1 4 1 2 3

3 2 1 1 2 3 2 1 4 5

1	IIII I	6
2	IIII	5
3	III	3
4	III	3
5	III	3

What is the median of the group?
The median is found by putting the numbers in order

1,1,1,1,1,1,2,2,2,2,|2,3,3,3,4,4,4,5,5,5

What is the mean of the group?
The mean is found by adding all the numbers and dividing by 20. $52 \div 20 = 2.6$
The mean is 2.6.

What is the mode?
1 appears most often.
The mode is 1.

What is the range of the group?
The range is found by taking the smallest number from the largest.
$5 - 2 = 3$
The range is 3.

1

6 4 6 8 5 2 1 0

5 3 3 2 7 4 3 5

4 5 3 0 0 1 2 3

What number is the mode of the above group?

What is the median of the group?

What is the mean of the group?

What is the range of the group?

2 In Robert's maths group of 12 students the test marks were 6, 13, 8, 15, 5, 7, 10, 14, 19, 16, 17 and 14. What was the mean of the marks?

Find the mode and the median. Which of the three averages is highest?

TARGET 2

Name: _____ Date: _____

I can use a tally chart to group information.

☐ ☐ ☐ ☐

TARGET 4

Name: _____ Date: _____

I can find the mean, median, mode, and range of a list of numbers.

☐ ☐ ☐ ☐

TARGET 1

Name: _____ Date: _____

I use a strategy to help me keep track when I am reading lists of numbers.

☐ ☐ ☐ ☐

TARGET 3

Name: _____ Date: _____

I understand what is meant by mean, median, mode and range.

☐ ☐ ☐ ☐

Positive and negative number

What is the problem? Most students have a reasonable grasp of what happens with whole numbers bigger than zero. Add them and they get bigger: multiply and they get bigger more quickly. Subtract from a number and it gets smaller: divide and the answer is less than at the beginning.

Negative number makes less obvious sense.

Where to start: About the only practical image that is in regular use that uses negative number is the **thermometer** and this can be used to help a student visualise and estimate the answer. He needs to get into the habit of drawing a quick number line, which he can use to track adding and subtracting when using negative number.

$$\longrightarrow$$

$$+$$

$$\underline{-10\ -9\ -8\ -7\ -6\ -5\ -4\ -3\ -2\ -1\ 0\ 1\ 2\ 3\ 4\ 5\ 6\ 7\ 8\ 9\ 10}$$

$$-$$

$$\longleftarrow$$

Adding the arrows and symbols will remind the student which way to go *before* he starts the operation, reinforcing his memory of the pattern.

(If a student is uncertain what to do, it can be helpful to use a calculator in conjunction with a number line. Once he has carried out one calculation he can see which direction to take and can then use the pattern to complete other examples.)

Where to next: Multiplying and Dividing

$+ \times + = +$	Same signs	$+ \div + = +$
$- \times - = +$	$+$	$- \div - = +$
$- \times + = -$	Opposite signs	$- \div + = -$
$+ \times - = -$	$-$	$+ \div - = -$

A slight change of language can help a student make sense of this. *Five lots of minus five:* write –5 on five small pieces of paper and you can add them together and see that you have –25. *Four lots of minus three:* write the –3 on four pieces of paper and it becomes apparent that you have –12.

Two minus signs together can be pictured pulling together to make a plus sign. (And, again, a calculator can be uses to check the outcome.)

Use concrete objects – counters in red (for +) and blue (for –). Let a student see that when the colours mix the answer will be negative, while solid colours give a positive answer. For example: $-4 \times 6 =$ *Put down four blue counters and six red ones. Opposite colours indicate a minus number answer.* $-4 \times 6 = -24$

Tip

Positive and negative number

Use two rulers. Keep one the right way up. Turn the other upside down and match up the points where the two rulers read zero. The rulers can be used as a number line from –15 to +15.

+
$\longrightarrow$

15 14 13 12 11 10 9 8 7 6 5 4 3 2 1 0

0 1 2 3 4 5 6 7 8 9 10 11 12 13 14 15

–
$\longleftarrow$

Have the rulers in front of you. Look at the question.

$$-4 + 8 =$$

Put your pencil on –4 and move it eight figures to the right as you count.

$$-4 - 3 =$$

Put your pencil on –4 and move it three figures to the left as you count.

Less than nothing

Draw a number line with arrows indicating + and –, or use two rulers to work out the temperature.

1 The temperature in Moscow is –12°C and the temperature in London is 8°C. What is the difference in temperature?

2 Yesterday morning it was –8°C in New York. In the afternoon it warmed up to 3°C. How many degrees warmer did it get?

3 During a power cut, a freezer warmed up from –14°C to –3°C. What was the difference in temperature?

4 a) –4 + 6   b) –6 – 4   c) 7 – 11

d) 9 – 16   e) –7 + 12   f) 12 – 16

5 Complete the chart below. The first one has been done for you.

–10 –9 –8 –7 –6 –5 –4 –3 –2 –1 0 1 2 3 4 5 6 7 8

Minimum temperature	Maximum temperature	Difference
–8°C	6°C	14°C
–2°C	7°C	
–18°C	–3°C	
–11°C	4°C	

When multiplying and dividing positive and negative number, remember: **same signs** *give a* **plus answer** *and* **opposite signs** *give a* **minus answer.**
e.g. –5 × 8 = –40, but –5 × –8 = 40.   –40 ÷ 5 = –8, but –40 ÷ –5 =8

6 a) 3 × 4   b) –3 × 4   c) –3 × –4

d) 3 × –4   e) 12 ÷ 4   f) –12 ÷ 4

g) 12 ÷ –4   h) –12 ÷ –4   i) –24 ÷ 8

j) –21 ÷ –7   k) 5 × 8   l) –5 × 8

Date: _____

Name: _____

TARGET 2

I can use a calculator to add and subtract positive and negative numbers.

☐ ☐ ☐ ☐

Date: _____

Name: _____

TARGET 4

I can multiply and divide positive and negative numbers.

☐ ☐ ☐ ☐

Date: _____

Name: _____

TARGET 1

I can use a number line to add and subtract positive and negative numbers.

☐ ☐ ☐ ☐

Date: _____

Name: _____

TARGET 3

I know that same signs give a positive answer and opposite signs give a negative answer.

☐ ☐ ☐ ☐

Ratio

What is the problem? Students cannot visualise what is meant by ratio. They learn it as a pen and paper skill without relating it to a concrete meaning.

Where to start: Work on ratio seems to focus very often on a) cakes, b) concrete and c) lottery winnings. It is much easier to picture when each part is seen as a share of a whole.

Concrete is made up of cement, sand and water in the ratio 1 : 3 : 2

Grid

Total number of shares: 6

cement	water	water
sand	sand	sand

So if you have 120 m³ of concrete,

Divide it into six shares – 120 ÷ 6 = 20 – each share will be 20 m³

3 will be sand   –   3 × 20   –   60 m³ will be sand

2 will be water   –   2 × 20   –   40 m³ will be water

1 will be cement   –   1 × 20   –   20 m³ will be cement

Ratios are always written in the same order as in the question

If the question says the ratio of sand: cement: water is 3:2:1, you must keep the *same order*, or your answer will be wrong.

Ratios, like fractions, are expressed in the lowest possible terms.

If I share £24 out and give Ahmed £9, Ben £12 and Clare £3, you could say I am sharing out in the ratio

$$9 : 12 : 3$$

but I can simplify this to   ÷3   ÷ 3   ÷3

$$3 : 4 : 1$$

which means the same thing.

Working with ratio

Draw up a grid (as on page 124) so that you can see how many shares make up the total. Then you could use your tables square to help you work out how much is in each share.

example

180 sweets are shared out between Ryan, Sally and Tom in the ratio
4 : 3 : 2. How many sweets does Tom get?
There are 4 + 3 + 2 shares altogether. That is 9 shares.
Each share is 180 ÷ 9 = 20.
Tom gets 2 shares. That is 20 × 2 = 40.
Tom gets 40 sweets.

1 £300 is shared out between Alan, Harry and Kate in the ratio
3 : 5 : 2. How much does Kate get?

2 The ingredients for pastry are flour and fat in the ratio 2:1.

If the pastry weighs 270 g, what is the weight of flour?

3 Express these ratios in their lowest possible terms.

a) 8 : 10 : 2   b) 1000 : 5000 : 2000

c) 25 : 35 : 15   d) 7 : 28 : 14

e) 3 : 8 : 6   f) 27 : 18 : 36

4 A sum of money is shared out between Ann, Ben, Chris and Debbie in the ratio 4 : 5 : 1 : 2.

If Chris gets £20, how much will Ben get?

How much money is there altogether?

2

Name: _____ Date: _____

TARGET

I know that the order of the ratio must be exactly the same as in the question.

☐ ☐ ☐ ☐

4

Name: _____ Date: _____

TARGET

I can express a ratio in its lowest terms.

☐ ☐ ☐ ☐

1

Name: _____ Date: _____

TARGET

I can add the number of shares and work out the value of one of them.

☐ ☐ ☐ ☐

3

Name: _____ Date: _____

TARGET

If I am given the value of one part of the ratio, I can work out the value of the others.

☐ ☐ ☐ ☐

Fractions

What is the problem? Fractions ask students to carry out a sequence of steps for reasons they do not understand. They also expect them to remember two very different techniques: addition/subtraction and multiplication/division. The vocabulary of working with fractions is complicated and the skill is used infrequently.

Where to start: Adding and subtracting fractions cries out for **concrete illustration**. A student who cannot see why you cannot add

$$\frac{3}{4} + \frac{1}{9} \text{ to get } \frac{4}{13}$$

can **see** from a concrete example that a quarter and a ninth are not the same thing and understand why they have to be broken up into the same size pieces before you can add them.

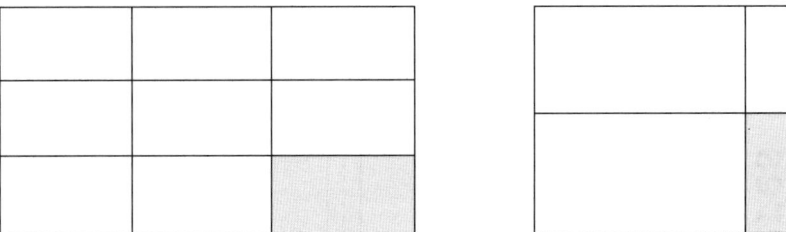

Do:

- Have him cut out fractions of all sizes from the same sized card: draw pizzas or chocolate bars and he will recognise that the pieces are not the same size.
- Help him to see that the bottom number of a fraction gives the total number of pieces needed to make a whole, and the top number is the pieces he has.
- Get him to think about where numbers meet on the tables square, so he can identify numbers that are common to both parts.
- Get him to make notes in his own words and put in pictures to reinforce his understanding.

Look! 12 is in the 3×
table and the 4×
table. That means I
can make ¼ and ⅓
into twelfths so I can
add them together.

1	2	3	4	5
2	4	6	8	10
3	6	9	12	15
4	8	12	16	20
5	10	15	20	25

● Remember that there is no guarantee that
  understanding the principle one day will enable
  him to remember it the next. It might be necessary
  to go back to the beginning every time.

Although some students grasp the way that whole
numbers in mixed fractions can be dealt with separately,
many simply find it confusing and prefer to turn mixed
fractions into top-heavy fractions. **Let them**. Trying to
change the way they work will knock what confidence
they have.

From fractions to decimals to percentages and back

This is a skill best recalled *visually*.

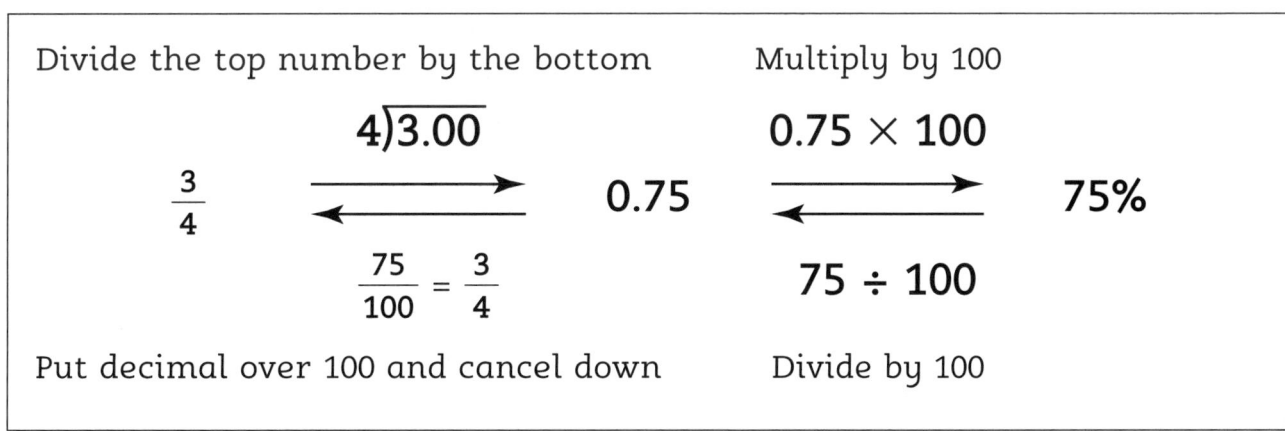

Divide the top number by the bottom   Multiply by 100

$\frac{3}{4}$ ⟶ $4\overline{)3.00}$ ⟶ 0.75   0.75 × 100 ⟶ 75%

$\frac{75}{100} = \frac{3}{4}$ 75 ÷ 100

Put decimal over 100 and cancel down   Divide by 100

Fractions in their lowest terms

When students are cancelling fractions to find their lowest terms, encourage them to use their tables square to find numbers that are factors of (go into) both figures.

If the numbers are too big, they should work through using the smallest possible number each time until they get to two numbers with no common factors.

$$\overset{\div 2}{} \quad \overset{\div 2}{} \quad \overset{\div 2}{} \quad \overset{\div 2}{} \quad \overset{\div 2}{}$$

$$\frac{96}{160} \quad \frac{48}{80} \quad \frac{24}{40} \quad \frac{12}{20} \quad \frac{6}{10} \quad \frac{3}{5}$$

$$\underset{\div 2}{} \quad \underset{\div 2}{} \quad \underset{\div 2}{} \quad \underset{\div 2}{} \quad \underset{\div 2}{}$$

If students work as far as possible with twos and threes, they are less likely to make mistakes.

Equivalent fractions

One half is the same as (equivalent to) two quarters.

$$\frac{96}{100} \text{ is the same as } \frac{3}{5}$$

$$\frac{1}{2} \text{ is the same as } \frac{3}{6}$$

$\frac{1}{6}$	$\frac{1}{6}$	$\frac{1}{6}$	$\frac{1}{6}$	$\frac{1}{6}$	$\frac{1}{6}$
$\frac{1}{2}$			$\frac{1}{2}$		

Fraction strips *(photocopiable resource 6)* are useful students relate the size of different fractions and to understand equivalent fractions

Where to next: multiplying and dividing fractions

Most students find multiplying and dividing fractions much more straightforward than adding and subtracting. Their main difficulty is remembering how to carry out a task they do not have to do very often. Learning to put arrows between the numbers can help.

$$\frac{3}{7} \times \frac{4}{5} = \frac{12}{35}$$

Nothing is a factor of both 12 and 35, so the fraction is expressed in its lowest terms.

If something is cancelled, it is crossed out.

Encourage students to exaggerate the multiplication sign so the arms of the cross show them which numbers can be divided by the same number to make the calculation easier.

$$\frac{\overset{1}{\cancel{5}}}{\underset{2}{\cancel{6}}} \times \frac{\overset{3}{\cancel{9}}}{\underset{4}{\cancel{20}}} = \frac{1}{2} \times \frac{3}{4} = \frac{3}{8}$$

When dividing fractions, which turns the second fraction upside down and then multiplies the two together: first write it out, use an arrow against the one that changes and proceed as for multiplication.

$$\frac{3}{5} \div \frac{3}{4} \quad \text{becomes} \quad \frac{\overset{1}{\cancel{3}}}{5} \times \frac{4}{\underset{1}{\cancel{3}}} = \frac{4}{5}$$

And make sure students know how to use their calculator to do fractions!

(See tips on using calculators, page 76–78.)

Working with fractions

Draw up the fractions so you can see their size when compared to each other. You can use a table square to find the smallest number that is common to both.

1

$\frac{1}{4}$

$\frac{1}{3}$

You cannot add ¼ to ⅓ because the pieces are not the same size. These have been broken down to make the pieces the same size. How many twelfths is the same as a quarter?

How many twelfths is the same as a third?

How many twelfths do you have if you add them together?

2 If you have half of one pizza and a quarter of another pizza, how much pizza do you have altogether?

3

$\frac{1}{4}$

$\frac{1}{8}$

Copy the shapes onto tracing paper and place them on top of each other.

How many pieces is the shape now divided into altogether?

How many pieces are now covered by the part marked ¼

Add all the shaded pieces together and write it down as a fraction of the total number of pieces.

Working with fractions

You can draw up the fractions so you can see their size when compared to each other, or you can use a table square to find the smallest number that is common to both.

1. Draw a circle round the equivalent fractions and join them together.

$\frac{1}{4}$	$\frac{3}{6}$	$\frac{4}{8}$	$\frac{2}{8}$	$\frac{5}{20}$	$\frac{25}{100}$
$\frac{1}{2}$	$\frac{4}{12}$	$\frac{3}{9}$	$\frac{7}{14}$	$\frac{12}{24}$	
$\frac{4}{16}$	$\frac{3}{12}$	$\frac{5}{15}$	$\frac{9}{18}$	$\frac{6}{24}$	$\frac{2}{6}$

2. Express ¾ as a decimal. What is ¾ expressed as a percentage?

3. Express ⅞ as a decimal. What is ⅞ expressed as a percentage?

4. What is 35% expressed as a decimal? What is 35% expressed as a fraction in its lowest terms?

5. Work out the answers. Remember to make the fractions into pieces that are the same size.

   a) $\frac{1}{4} + \frac{1}{2} =$ b) $\frac{1}{3} + \frac{2}{5} =$

   c) $\frac{3}{4} - \frac{1}{3} =$ d) $\frac{7}{8} - \frac{3}{5} =$

6. Work out the answers.

   a) $\frac{1}{2} \times \frac{2}{3} =$ b) $\frac{4}{5} \times \frac{3}{4} =$

   c) $\frac{3}{4} \div \frac{1}{2} =$ d) $\frac{5}{9} \div \frac{2}{3} =$

TARGET 1

Name: _____ Date: _____

I can put fractions in the same sized pieces so I can add or subtract them.

☐ ☐ ☐ ☐

TARGET 2

Name: _____ Date: _____

I can recognise equivalent fractions and express fractions in their lowest terms.

☐ ☐ ☐ ☐

TARGET 3

Name: _____ Date: _____

I am confident that I can multiply fractions.

☐ ☐ ☐ ☐

TARGET 4

Name: _____ Date: _____

I am confident that I can divide fractions.

☐ ☐ ☐ ☐

Algebra

What is the problem? Take away the numbers and replace them with letters and many students immediately lose control. After all, algebra is hard, isn't it? Some students just do not believe that they can 'do' algebra.

Actually, most of the skills required by students who find mathematics a real problem are not really that hard at all, as long as they can make sense of what they are doing.

Where to start:

● Problem 1: *Leaving out the multiplication sign*. Start by including it, but insist that it is always written in a **different colour**, so that it can be seen that it is **not** an *x*. After a while, when the student is bored with having to change his pen, suggest that, actually, it could be left out, and he could just **assume** that when letters and numbers are written next to each other, there would be a multiplication sign.

$4 \times x \times y$ would become $4xy$

So:- $3 \times p \times q \times r$ – would be what?

$9 \times a \times b \times g \times h$ – would be what?

● Problem 2: **Simplifying**. Use concrete objects of different colours, such as cubes or counters, to represent what is being simplified.

$2b + 3b + 5g - 4b - 2g + 4b$

Separate the different letters – (*you could imagine that the letters are colours.*)

◪□ + ◪◪◪ + □□□□ = □□□□□

2 blue cubes plus 3 blue cubes minus 4 blue cubes plus 4 blue cubes = 5 blue cubes

$$2b + 3b + 5g - 4b - 2g + 4b = 5b + 3g$$

5 green cubes minus 2 green cubes = 3 green cubes

$$\square\square\square\cancel{\square}\cancel{\square} = \square\square\square$$

So you are left with $5b + 3g$. A student can move on to using pieces of paper to use this technique in an examination.

So: Use coloured blocks or pieces or paper to simplify this

$$3a + 2a + 4b - 2b - a$$

Now simplify this:

$$9d + 3d + 6m - 2d + 5m - 2m$$

- Problem 3: **Solve the equation**. Students usually work either by using the balance method, or by 'moving across the equals sign and changing the sign'. Build up confidence slowly, and be prepared to revert to using concrete objects each time you revisit the skill.

$$3f + 4 = 2f + 9$$

① take off 4   ② take off 4 to keep it balanced

$$3f + 4 - 4 = 2f + 9 - 4$$

$$3f = 2f + 5$$

④ take off 2f to keep it balanced   ③ take off 2f

$$3f - 2f = 2f - 2f + 5$$

$$f = 5$$

Remind student visually that to keep equations balanced, the **same thing** has to be done to **both sides**. Again, this can be done using **coloured counters** or **blocks** and a **balance**.

- The number of counters representing the letter can be concealed by slipping them in a small envelope.

136

- The student can place three packets and four counters on one side and two packets plus nine counters on the other.
- If he takes four counters from each side the scales will balance.
- If he then removes two packets from each side, the scales will balance.
- He will end up with one packet on one side and five separate counters on the other. When checked, he will find that the packet contains five counters.

Where to next: Rearranging formulae

One way to help a student reorganise information is to go back to using the 'machine'. If he has to work out what is done to turn y into x, he can then reverse the machine to find out what is done to x to turn it into y. *When in reverse, the signs change to their opposite.* This is using the student's patterning skill to walk through a procedure.

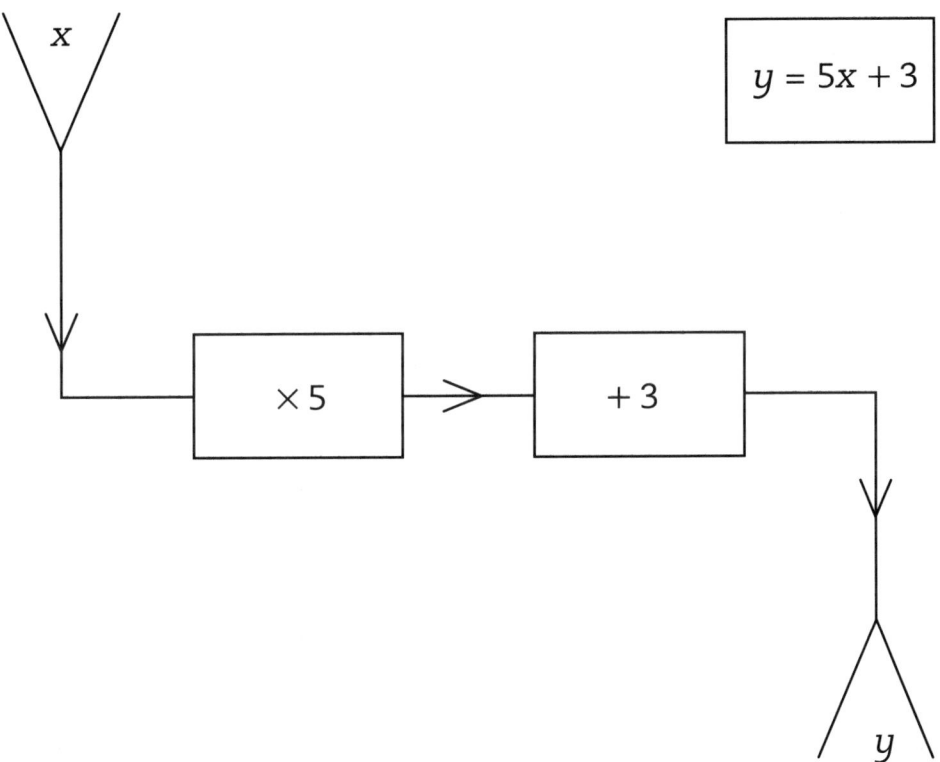

The student works through the problem step-by-step in a visual way.

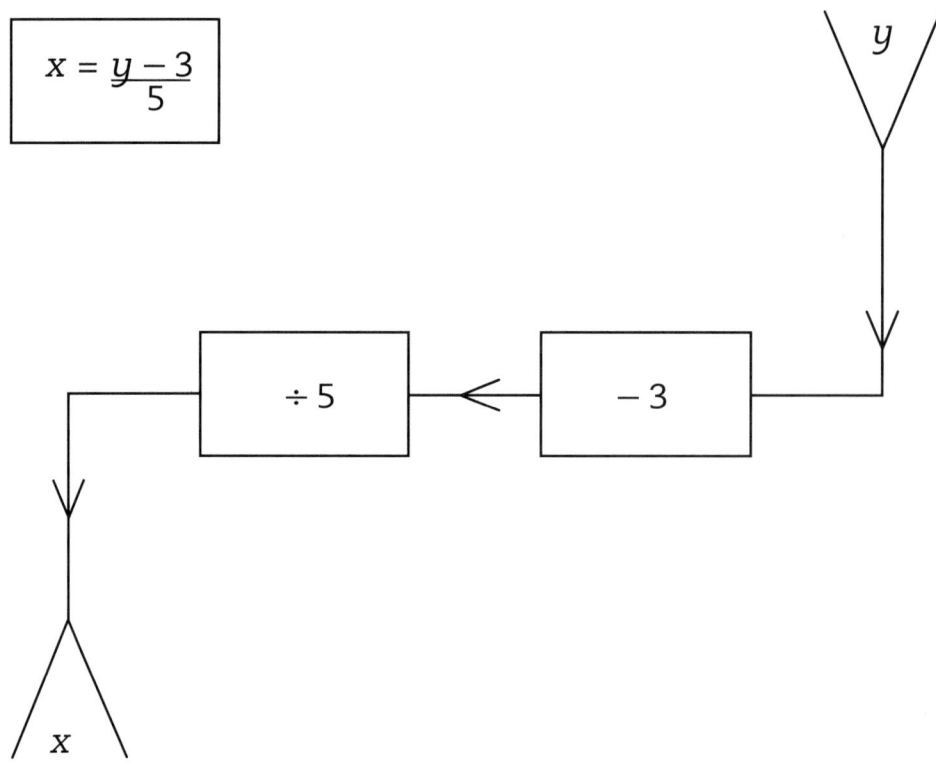

$$x = \frac{y - 3}{5}$$

This method of working is very commonly used when students begin working with formulae, but is usually abandoned rapidly as they 'understand' what to do. Continue to suggest students use machines. *They work.*

Extending machines

Once a student is confident with the skill involved in using a machine, he can dispense with the need to draw one and use a grid.

$y = 5x + 3$

x	0	1	2	3
×5	0	5	10	15
+3	+3	+3	+3	+3
y	3	8	13	18

With a grid, he can work out the value of y for any value of x.

Finding the formula

This task comes in a variety of forms. The first is when a student is given a short passage to read:

'Jack's Plumbing' charges customers £35 per hour for their services together with a £50 call-out charge. Write the cost as a formula with C being cost and h being hour.

This kind of question is more a question of **decoding** language rather than one of using algebra. Students need to **talk through** the meaning and practise with lots of similar questions until they recognise the type of question. Use **PACES** (*photocopiable resources sheet 10*) to visualise the task and consider the different elements. Vocalise the problem.

He can break down the information given:

Every customer has to pay £50.
The charge is £35 for each hour.
The cost is going to be £35 times the number of hours plus the call-out charge.
I could write that as:

$$C = 35h + 50$$

And that is really all there is to it.

Working with letters

Use cubes or counters to help you visualise what it is you are trying to do, or draw out the problem on the paper in front of you.

1 Simplify: (example $c + c + c + t - c = 2c + t$)

a) $a + a + a + a$ b) $a + a + b + a$

c) $s + t + s + t + t - v$ d) $3m + 2m + 2p - p$

2 Simplify: (example $7 \times a \times b = 7ab$)

a) $4 \times a \times b$ b) $5 \times g \times h$

c) $b \times d \times n$ d) $c \times 5 \times d$

3 Work out the answer if x = 4

(example $3x - 2 = 3 \times 4 - 2 = 10$)

a) $2x + 1$ b) $x - 2$

c) $3x - 5$ d) $10x + 5$

4 Work out the answer if $g = 3$ and $h = 5$

a) $2g + h$ b) $g + 2h$

c) $3g - h$ d) $2gh$

e) $\dfrac{4gh}{2h}$ f) $g^2 + h^2$

5 Use the balance method to work out the value of x.

● Example $2x + 3 = 11$.

● *Take 3 from each side.* $(2x + 3 - 3 = 11 - 3) = 2x = 8$.

● *Divide both sides by 2.* $(2x \div 2 = 8 \div 2) = x = 4$

a) $x + 5 = 8$ b) $2x + 3 = 7$

c) $4x - 6 = 14$ d) $3x - 3 = 18$

Working with letters

Task 1. Use the balance method to work out the value of x.

Task 2. Read the questions carefully and note down what you are being told. You can draw a machine to work out what happens.

Task 1: **Example:**

$$2x - 3 = x + 1$$

$$2x - 3 + 3 = x + 1 + 3$$

$$2x = x + 4$$

$$2x - x = x - x + 4$$

$$x = 4$$

---

1 a) $4x - 3 = 3x$ b) $7x + 2 = 5x + 4$
      c) $5x - 2 = 3x + 3$ d) $10x - 8 = 8x - 2$

Task 2: **Example:** *Fix-It charges £60 to all customers for examining their computers. Then the firm charges £45 per hour for labour. Write an expression that shows the cost of repair, with C as cost and h representing hours.*

The cost is £45 times the number of hours plus the £60 charge
$$C = 45h + 60.$$

---

2 For a wedding reception, a restaurant charges £25 per guest plus a booking charge of £100. Write the cost as an expression, with **C** as the cost and **g** representing guests.
Tom and Mia have invited 45 guests. How much will the reception cost?

3 Kelly earns £200 per week. If she works overtime she earns an £7 per hour. Write an expression to show her earnings, with **E** as earnings and **o** as overtime.
One week she works 10 hours overtime. How much does she earn?
Another week she earns £249. How many hours overtime does she work?

2

Name: _____ Date: _____

TARGET

I can substitute numbers for letters and work out the answer.

☐ ☐ ☐ ☐

4

Name: _____ Date: _____

TARGET

I can find a rule and put it into an expression.

☐ ☐ ☐ ☐

1

Name: _____ Date: _____

TARGET

I can group similar terms.

☐ ☐ ☐ ☐

3

Name: _____ Date: _____

TARGET

I can rearrange equations to find the value of x.

☐ ☐ ☐ ☐

Target Maths – Skills Area 3: The School Curriculum

Shape – Helping Students Remember and Understand Shape

Shape is a huge topic that students are introduced to over most of their school life. It includes 2D shapes, 3D shapes, lines, angles, symmetry and congruence and transformations. To further complicate the topic the student has to apply calculations, graphing, measurement skills and facts to **shape**. In this section we review shape from its basic principles to give students a starting point to access the shape related topics in the curriculum.

What's the problem? One problem often identified is the specialised language connected with shape. There are a lot of unfamiliar words connected with the topic which can cause some confusion. The students' understanding appears fragmented and they may never make connections between previously learnt work and new work.

Where to start? The students cannot make calculations involving graphs or shapes unless they are confident with shapes, so it is necessary to start at the beginning to build a secure base for their understanding.

Shapes are formed by lines and angles, so the suggested sequence of learning is:

Lines $\longrightarrow$ angles $\longrightarrow$ 2D shape $\longrightarrow$ 3D shape.

Moving on to symmetry, transformations and measurements.

The sequence lines, angles, 2D shape and 3D shape is meant to be taught **quickly** and **sequentially** to allow the student to build up an understanding of the shape system.

Lines: There are many different types of lines but there are two important pieces of knowledge about lines.

1   **Parallel lines** form a key feature in shape. The student needs to know what **parallel** means and be able to recognise them in a variety of formats.

2   **Markings** on lines causes confusion, the student needs to recognise and interpret these markings.

The student needs to know:

>> refers to parallel   // refers to size

Initially use **colour** for markings.

- To increase a student's level of skills, give him a sheet of lines and shapes and ask him to mark them.
- To increase a student's skill level, give him a sheet of marked lines and shapes and ask him to explain the markings.
- To increase a younger student's skill level, give him a pad of stickers and ask him to go round the room and identify lines that are parallel or the same size.

Angles: Many students describe angles as 'something they do in maths'.

To start: understanding that an angle is a turn.

- Help the student to identify an angle as a 'turn'.
- Next identify static angles that they might find in the classroom.
- Then identify situations where angles may be continually changing: an example to use is an aeroplane. Use a paper aeroplane and get the student to demonstrate the stages of runway, take off, and flight to show how the angle of the plane changes.

Moving on: The next stage is to measure the angle, as it is the size that gives its type and name.

What tool to use and what units of measurement? The student needs to know the unit of measure is the degree and its symbol.

Use a clock face or angle dial which has been split into 36 parts and which has two hands the same size. *(Photocopiable resource sheet 11)*

When using the angle dial it is important to identify:

- The point of turn
- That one hand will stay still while the other moves.

First ask the student to demonstrate a small or big turn.

Next ask him to make an angle and count the degrees in tens starting at zero. This is good preparation for using the protractor.

Move on quickly to identifying the three main angles.

Note that an angle is identified first by its size and then its name. Often a student may have difficulty if asked to identify an acute angle, but he can show an angle less than 90°. The relationship between the angles is based on their size.

Start with the **main angles**

- 360° full turn
- 180° straight line
- 90° quarter turn or right angle.

Move on to the **special angles**:

- Less than 90° acute
- More than 90° but less than 180° obtuse
- More than 180° but less than 360° reflex.

When the student has got to this stage he is ready to **use a protractor** to measure and draw angles. As before, **the student has to be familiar with the tool before he can use it to measure.**

Use a clear plastic protractor as it is easier to read and, wherever possible, a complete 360° protractor as this allows the student to connect angles to the angle dial. (*photocopiable resource sheet 11.*)

If a full protractor is available, start by asking the student to compare it to his angle dial.

Hints – **using a protractor to measure**.

- Make sure the lines of the angle are long enough for the protractor.
- Estimate the angle, more or less than 90°.
- Decide on the point of turn.
- Decide on the base line.
- Find zero.

Do not read the scale but count the turn in tens, starting from zero.
This prevents the most common error of reading the wrong scale.

Hints – **using a protractor to draw an angle**.

- Sketch an estimate of the angle.
- Identify the angle on the protractor.
- Draw the base line.
- Match points of turn.
- Draw the angle and compare to sketch.

Moving on – The next stage in the sequence is for the **lines and angles** to come together to form **shapes**.

Shapes can be made with straight lines or curved lines, but in this section we are working with shapes with straight lines.

Where to start? Give the student knowledge by showing him all the shapes, from 3 sided to 10 sided.

Shapes are connected by the number of sides rather than their names, so start with the number.

3   triangle

4   quadrilateral

> *Hint*
>
> To decide the name of a shape, count the sides.
>
> At this point the student needs to be introduced to the idea of regular and irregular shapes.

5   pentagon

6   hexagon

7   heptagon

8   octagon

9   nonagon

10   decagon

The student needs to concentrate on **triangles** and **quadrilaterals**. The work needs to be supported with carefully marked illustrations. A useful strategy is to give the student a set of cards A4 size that they can use to collect information about shapes. They will need about 10 pieces of card. The student should be given the blank cards and build up the information on the cards as he is introduced to the various topics of lines, angles, symmetry, perimeter, area and volume. Examples of completed shape resource cards are shown on the *photocopiable sheets 12a, 12b. (The student would begin with blank cards.)*

Triangles

Do:

Start by reminding students that triangles are made with **lines** and **angles** and they have three lines and three angles. They need to apply their knowledge of lines and angles to triangles.

> **Activity**
>
> Give the student marked triangles and ask him to name them and explain his answer.
>
> Give him a name of a triangle and ask him to draw a rough sketch and put in the facts that make it that kind of triangle.

Triangles with angles and sides all equal are **equilateral**.
Triangles with a 90° angle are **right angle** triangles.
Triangles with 2 angles and 2 sides equal are **isosceles** triangles.
Triangles with all sides and angles different are **scalene** triangles.
The last fact that the students need to know is:

Angles of a triangle add up to 180°.

● If time allows get the student to prove this fact by cutting up the triangle and placing the angles on a straight line, as demonstrated below.

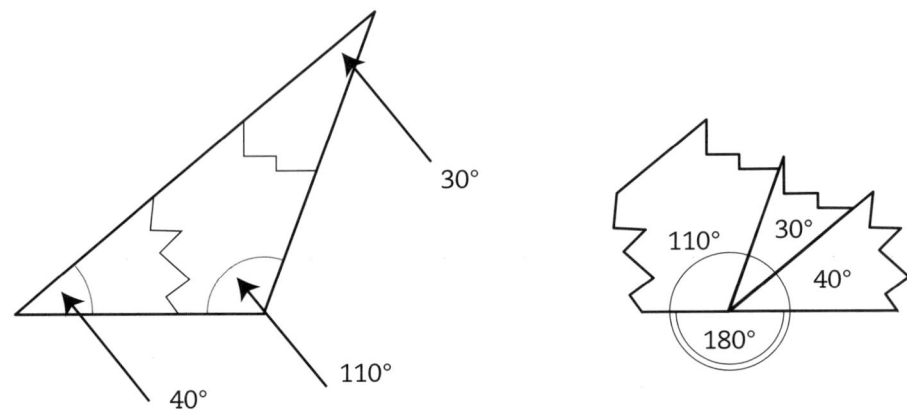

- Conclude this section on triangles by giving the student the information cards to make. He should draw his triangle in the middle and print its name clearly inside the shape. He can then use this as the focal point for a mind map of the different facts about triangles. A4 card is used to give space to add more information on symmetry, perimeter, and area.

- When making these cards, **colour code** the information, as this makes it very easy to refer to them. A sample is demonstrated on *photocopiable sheet 12a.*

Quadrilaterals

- Start in the same way by reminding the student that quadrilaterals are made with lines and angles: they have four lines and four angles. He needs to apply his knowledge of lines and angles to quadrilaterals.

Activity

Give each student marked quadrilaterals and ask him to name them and explain his answer.

Give him a name and ask them to draw a rough sketch and mark the attributes (identifying points).

Square: all angles are 90° and all sides are equal.
Rectangles: all angles are 90° but only opposite sides are equal.
Rhombus: angles are **not** 90°, but opposite angles are equal. All sides are the same size.
Parallelogram: angles are **not** 90° but opposite angles are equal, and only opposite sides are equal.

- Now get students to make A4 information cards for each quadrilateral. Once again these can be added to later.

3D shape

The starting point for the students is to be able to:

- Identify attributes
- Name the shapes
- Identify the net of the shape

To start

- Remind students of using lines and angles to classify 2D shape.
- Give the student some regular 3D shapes.
- Work with the student draw up the list of attributes that can be used to classify 3D shape.

The 3 attributes are:

- faces
- edges
- vertices

Moving on

- Give the student a selection of regular 3D shape and help him to put them into groups. These groups could be with flat surfaces, with curved surfaces, coming to a point or with straight sides. The student needs to identify cubes, spheres, cuboids, prisms, pyramids, cylinders and cones.
- Ask the student to make a chart showing the attributes of the plastic models.

The student needs to end up with a match between the key attributes and the names of the 3D shapes.

Moving on further

The next activity can be very difficult for many students, but it is the situation in which they will find themselves when working with textbooks and in exams. They have to identify key attributes and name shapes using 2D images of 3D models.

To start

- Ask student to match 2D pictures to 3D models.
- Give the student only the pictures and ask him to identify the attributes and names.

Moving on

Get the student to build a set of models using pre-printed nets. This can be time consuming but is a very useful way to help the student to build up his mental images and also to work directly with the attributes of faces, vertices and edges.

Activity 1

Give the student a set of models, 2D images and nets and ask him to match them and name them.

Activity 2

Give the student a 3D models and a net with a part missing. Can he identify the problem?

Activity 3

Give the student a 3D model and ask him to sketch the net.

As a source of reference the student should continue to build up his resource cards to include 3D shapes. Each one should have a picture of the shape, a net of the shape, and a summary of the shapes attributes. Later information relating to the shapes surface area, volume or planes of symmetry can be added. (*Photocopiable resource sheet 12b.*)

Symmetry

This topic involves reflective symmetry, rotational symmetry and plane symmetry.

Use regular shapes as this reinforces and extends the knowledge students already have.

This topic is very easy for some students and extremely difficult for others. Where students are having difficulty and cannot visualise or move the shape in their mind, they have to be given a strategy to move the shape physically.

Getting started

Activity 1

To find the lines of symmetry in regular shapes.

Give the student a sheet of regular shapes, ask him to cut them out and demonstrate that he can fold them over to identify a line of symmetry. He should search for the lines of symmetry in each of the regular shapes. Once this is done he can add this information to the shape fact cards.

Activity 2

To find lines of symmetry by tracing.

The student should then be given another set of shapes that he cannot cut out, but he can trace them, cut out the tracing and then fold it. It should be pointed out that this is a strategy he can use in an exam, as tracing paper is always available.

Activity 3

To draw in the second half of a shape.

The student should be given a sheet of half shapes and be asked to complete these. He should again use his tracing strategy, but needs to remember to flip the tracing over. One way to help him to remember to flip the shape is to lightly colour the tracing and the coloured side has to be next to the paper.

2

Name: _____ Date: _____

TARGET

I can recognise acute, obtuse, reflex and right angles and measure them with a protractor.

☐ ☐ ☐ ☐

4

Name: _____ Date: _____

TARGET

I can use tracing paper to help me find reflective and rotational symmetry.

☐ ☐ ☐ ☐

1

Name: _____ Date: _____

TARGET

I know what is meant by parallel lines and can recognise the markings that tell me when lines are parallel.

☐ ☐ ☐ ☐

3

Name: _____ Date: _____

TARGET

I have made revision cards that give the facts related to different 2D and 3D shapes.

☐ ☐ ☐ ☐

Area and volume

What is the problem? A student who has grasped the different shapes and can list the points that make a trapezium and rectangle different can still become confused by trying to remember how to work out area and volume.

Where to start: Some students find it helpful to use different **colours** for each of the formulae for area – and to write the formula on top of the **shape**, which is shaded in the same colour. Then, when trying to remember the formula, they can **picture** the shape and link it with the instructions in the same colour.

Area is working out how much can fit into two dimensions – that is why the answer is always in units^2

A student's exercise book looks tidy when written neatly in blue ink – but the single colour can mask the information a student is trying to recall.

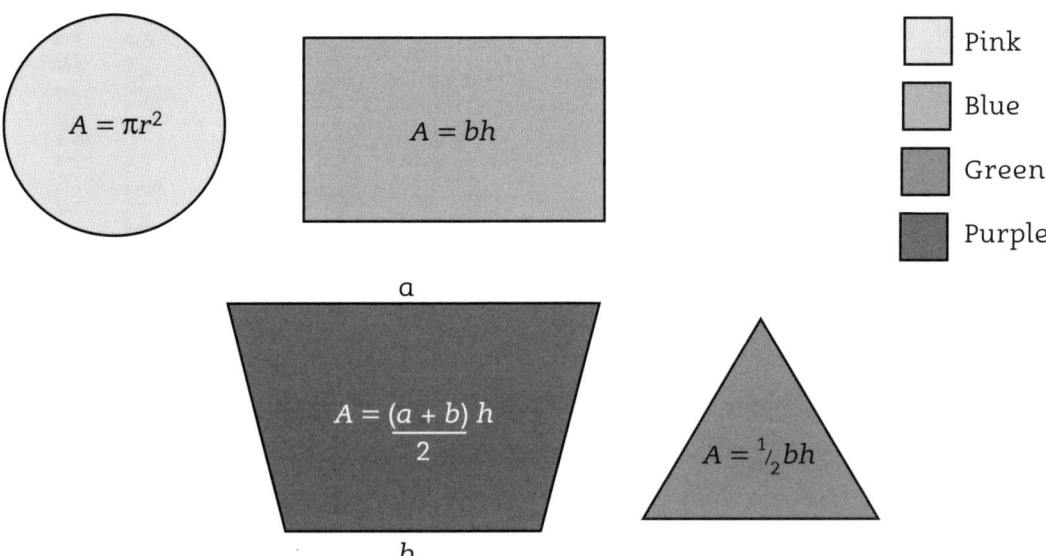

$A = \pi r^2$

$A = bh$

Pink
Blue
Green
Purple

a

$A = \dfrac{(a + b)\, h}{2}$

$A = {}^1/_2 bh$

b

(Do not forget that this technique will be useless if the student cannot recall the meaning of symbols like π, or forgets what the letters **b**, or **h**, or **r** represent. Write formulae out in *words* as well as using *pictures*. The student can use **visualisation** to remember what the image looks like and verbalisation to add meaning to it.)

Volume is about working out how much fits into three dimensions – which is why the answer is in units^3

Use concrete equipment to reinforce the idea of *capacity*. Glasses, cake tins, empty cans – borrow measuring tubes. Fit cubes into boxes. It is very difficult for students to imagine three dimensions without plenty of practical experience of linking the **ideas** and the **terms**.

Where to next: As a student learns new information about shape, area and volume, he needs to remember to update his **shape resource cards**, so that he has a reference sheet available to him at all times. (See *photocopiable resource sheets 12a and 12b*.)

Working with area

Area is flat. *Draw the shapes to help picture the area. Write down the rule and think about the meaning before you start to work out the answer. Put in a dotted line to show the height of shapes. Remember units are written as units^2.*

1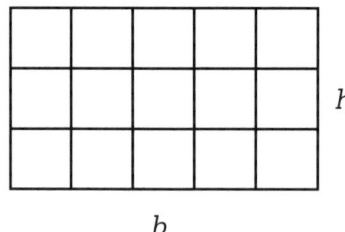

A rectangle has a base 5 m long and a height of 3 m. How many m^2 is the shape?

2 A rectangle has a base of 8 cm and a height of 5 cm. What area does it cover?

3 The formula for finding the area of a triangle is half the base times height. What is the area of this right-angled triangle?

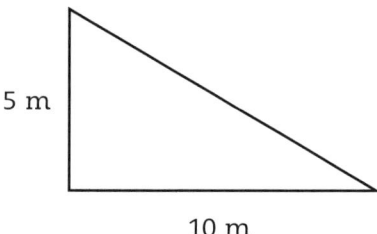

4 Match the shape to the formula to find its area.

Shape	Formula
triangle	bh
circle	bh
rectangle	πr^2
trapezium	$\frac{1}{2}bh$
parallelogram	$\frac{1}{2}(a + b)\,h$

Sketch each shape and write the formula in the middle.

Working with volume

Volume is three dimensional. *Picture the shape as a real container and think about how much can go inside. Write down the rule and think about what it means. Remember that units are written as units³.*

1

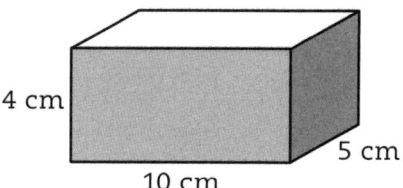

4 cm

10 cm

5 cm

If John fills the bottom of this box with cubes that are 1 cm², how many cubes will fill one layer?

How many cubes altogether will fill the four layers?

2

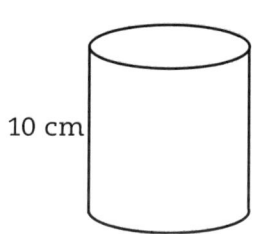

10 cm

The radius of the can is 5 cm. If Tom finds the area of the end, using the formula $A = \pi r^2$, and multiplies it by the length, he will discover the volume of the can in cm³. (Use 3.14 as π)

What is the volume of the can?

What is the name given to this kind of shape?

Write in words what you have to do to find the volume of this shape. See if you can write it as a formula.

3 Explain what is meant by a prism. Why does the area of the end of a prism together with its length give you its volume?

2

Name: _____ Date: _____

TARGET

I can use a strategy to help me remember the rules for finding the area of different shapes.

☐ ☐ ☐ ☐

4

Name: _____ Date: _____

TARGET

I can break shapes down into smaller parts to help me work out their area and volume.

☐ ☐ ☐ ☐

1

Name: _____ Date: _____

TARGET

I understand that area is two dimensional and volume is three dimensional.

☐ ☐ ☐ ☐

3

Name: _____ Date: _____

TARGET

I can use a strategy to help me remember how to find the volume of different shapes.

☐ ☐ ☐ ☐

Data Handling

What is the problem? A student is asked to manipulate large quantities of information and do a variety of things at once. His memory is often overloaded and he can make mistakes that he could avoid. He needs to work through the stages of **PACES** (*photocopiable resource 10*) or, at a simpler level, become a **STUD** (*photocopiable resource 9*).

Where to start:

Tally charts

- It is usually easier for a student to read **down a column** rather than **across a row**.
- Use a ruler, set square or a simple piece of paper to isolate the column being copied.
- Spend extra time ensuring that the **first groups** are correct when working out group values. The rest follow the pattern.
- Add the frequency and check you have the right number of values recorded.

Pie charts

- The total number of things or people tallied (the frequency) has to be made to match the number of degrees in a circle. Look at the common frequencies used in questions and start by working out what multiple needs to be used.

Common multiples

36	×	10
45	×	8
90	×	4
120	×	3

Graphs

- A major area of difficulty many students have with drawing graphs is that they rush into the task without spending enough time thinking about the scale on the axes. They need to *s-l-o-w d-o-w-n* and think about how many squares they are going to use to represent their figures.

- This also causes a problem when it comes to reading information on graphs. (This is particularly true when reading Speed, Time, Distance graphs, where the x axis usually represents time. One small box of ten squares usually represents one hour – therefore, each small square represents one tenth of an hour – $60 \div 10 = 6$, so each small square equals 6 minutes. If a student knows this, he will be more successful in reading the graph.)
- **Students should always put their pencils down and work out the scale of the axes before starting to work on inputting or reading the information.**
- Then, they need to use a SHARP pencil, and a RULER.

Scales

Many students experience difficulty with reading, creating and marking scales. They have difficulty understanding the information on a scale and find it difficult to interpret the information identified by the pointer. In this section we suggest strategies to try to help students understand scales, to develop their skills in using scales, and to develop their skills to design scales to fit data.

What is the problem? Scales are in use in many different circumstances, with many different tools and using many different units. The students fail to recognise the common features and are asked to apply them to problems before they are skilled in using them. Rarely are students simply given practice in reading and marking scales.

Where to start?

What is the purpose of scales?
What are the common features of scales?
What information is written on a scale?
What are the most common types of scales?

What measuring tool to use? The most appropriate tool is again the number line. The student is already familiar number lines and they can be used for every type of scale.

Getting started Purpose – The student needs to know that scales are used for measuring.

Common features:

- Scales are patterns.
- The pattern repeats itself
- Scale will increase in one direction and will decrease in the other direction.

Information – The scale should always contain information about the units being used.

Types of scales; length, mass, capacity, temperature.

Task 1

Get the student to identify the patterns of the scale and the intervals.

For example:

Get the student to practise using practical examples, such as thermometers and speedometers.

Task 2

Model to the student how you might design a scale on any straight line. Explain clearly what your pattern will be and write on the numbers.

Give the student a piece of blank paper. Ask him to draw three lines from the top to the bottom of the paper. Ask him to design three different scales and write on the numbers.

Task 3

Give the student some squared paper and ask him to repeat task 2. Encourage him to use the squares as a guide for the class intervals.

Task 4

Give the student some samples of graph paper. Discuss the intervals of the grid on the paper. Ask him to design sets of scales on the graph paper.

Moving on The student should now be able to identify the patterns in a scale and the value of the divisions between the class intervals. He now needs to investigate scales on measuring tools he might use in the real world. The most obvious place to start is to use his own ruler.

What can he see?

- The pattern goes up in single units.
- There are 10 divisions between each number.
- The halfway point, 5, is marked with a longer line.
- The scale is marked in **cm**.

Where to next? Before moving on the student needs to collect some facts about the scales he might need to use and he needs to revise his units of measure.

Length – millimetre, centimetre, metre and kilometre.
Mass – grams and kilograms
Capacity – millilitres and litres.
Temperature – degrees centigrade

- Give the student the real tools (e.g. thermometer, timer) and ask him to explain the scale to you. Using the 'real thing' has the most impact.
- Give the student pictures of the scale as you might find in a textbook (Resource sheet 14) and ask him to explain them to you.

Where to next? Develop the student's ability to design scales.

Give him some graph paper and some tasks to complete.

- Draw a set of axes that go from 0 to 20 and the scale is 1:2.
- Draw a set of axes that go from 0 to 100 and the scale is 1:10. Mark in the mid points.
- Draw a set of axes that go from 0 to 30 and the scale is 1:5

The student should now be able to design a scale, identify what the pattern of the values will be and say what the division will be. The next step is to design a scale for a specific set of data.

The most likely situation where this will be required is to design a scale on a set of axes. So this is the format in which the practice will take place.

Where to start? **LOOK** at the data. What is the lowest value? What is the highest value?

LOOK at your graph paper. What is the pattern and what are the divisions?

You are looking for the best fit.

Demonstrate the first practice question to the student. Then ask him to try the rest working independently, use the photocopiable worksheet Designing Scales, p 165.

The most important practice the student can be given now is to use his skills with scales and apply them to measurement, graph or data handling problems in his school text book.

Designing scales

1. Here is a set of data showing the temperature in the first eight weeks of summer.

Week	1	2	3	4	5	6	7	8
Temperature	27	30	31	30	33	34	35	37

Draw a set of axes putting the temperature on the vertical axis and the weeks on the horizontal axis.

2. Here is a set of data showing the number of ice-creams sold by the school tuck shop last year.

Month	Jan	Feb	Mar	April	May	June	July	Aug	Sept	Oct	Nov	Dec
Number sold	23	19	29	71	49	97	93	99	81	63	26	3

Draw a set of axes putting the number sold on the vertical axis and the months on the horizontal axis.

3. Here is a set of data showing the results of a science experiment. A liquid was heated and then allowed to cool. The temperature was taken every five minutes.

Time	0	5	10	15	20	25	30	35	40	45	50	55
Temp	35	40	55	60	85	100	75	60	60	55	45	30

Draw a set of axes putting the temperature on the vertical axis and the time on the horizontal axis.

4. Draw a set of axes that could be used to plot a conversion graph. The graph will show the relationship between age and height. The age range will go from 10 – 20 years and the height range will go from 1.30 m to 1.90 m.

5. A doctor wants to plot mass against age so the he can track children's weight. Design a set of axes that he could use with an age range of 5 – 18 and a weight range of 20 kg – 90 kg.

TARGET 1

Name: _____ Date: _____

I have developed strategies to make my tally charts accurate.

☐ ☐ ☐ ☐

TARGET 2

Name: _____ Date: _____

I know how to work out the angle for each value in a pie chart.

☐ ☐ ☐ ☐

TARGET

Name: _____ Date: _____

I understand how to work out scales and read the intervals accurately.

☐ ☐ ☐ ☐

TARGET

Name: _____ Date: _____

I spend time working out the values on the axes of a graph before I draw or read it.

☐ ☐ ☐ ☐

Time – applying time skills to timetables

In senior school the most common maths problem that a student will have to deal with involves timetables.

> What facts does the student need to learn?
> What tools does he have he can use?

The student needs to be familiar with the 24 hour clock and the 'time line'. Both of these are dealt with under time in Skills Area 2, page 93.

How to prepare the student: To prepare the student he needs to apply the time line tool to a timetable. As always make sure the student is efficient in using the tool before he is asked to apply it to a problem-solving situation. The second step in the preparation is making sure he understands the format of timetables. They can be very confusing as timetables are complex.

Applying timetables to 'time line': Begin with a timetable with which the student is familiar. The TV schedule is a good starting point. The first task is to convert it to a time line. Ask the student to look at the model on photocopiable sheet 5a and then give him a TV schedule and let him practise.

Reading timetables: The next step is to introduce the student to a more complicated timetable such as a bus timetable. Some time will have to be spent investigating the format and reading the information. These are often set out as two way tables and the student may need practice in reading the information. A selection of practice reading exercises is on the worksheet **Reading Timetables**. This can be completed orally. It should be enhanced by giving the student a commercial timetable and asking questions.

Activity

An addition activity is to have two different timetables and:

- Spot the similarities
- Spot the differences

Which is more user friendly and why?

Activity

An activity to help understanding and fluency in reading time tables is to have two copies of time tables and take turns between student and teacher to ask questions.

In order to be able to answer a question, the student now has to extract information from a timetable. He should now be able to plot the information on a 'time line'. If this is so, then he is ready to use his skills in problem solving situations.

In the first problem the student should complete a perfect neat example as this will be the model to approach other problems. (See photocopiable sheet **Calculating with Timetables**, (page 170)).

Reading timetables

The questions should be asked as **an oral exercise** to help familiarise the student with reading timetables.

This is a timetable for the 54 bus which goes from Rose Bay to Hillhead.

Rose Bay	0905	1005	1105	1205	1305	1405
Bourne	0925	1025	–	–	1325	1425
Troy	1015	1115	–	–	1415	1515
Kirby	1030	–	1210	–	1430	1530
Cox Green	1055	–	1235	–	–	1555
Hillhead	1135	1220	1315	1355	1530	1635

1. Where does the first bus of the day start?

2. How many times does it stop?

3. Where is the last stop?

4. How many times a day does a bus run from Rose Bay?

5. Is there a pattern to the departure times?

6. Is there a pattern to the arrival times at Hillhead?

7. Why is the pattern to the arrival times different?

8. Without calculating, which bus do you think will be the quickest and why?

9. Which two buses take the longest to get from Rose Bay to Hillhead?

10. How many stops does the bus leaving at 1105 make after leaving Rose Bay?

11. Which bus makes no stops between Rose Bay and Hillhead?

12. If I want to arrive at Hillhead at 1530 what time do I need to leave Rose Bay?

13. I go to college in Rose Bay and I finish college at 1330. Which bus will I catch to go home to Hillhead?

Calculating with timetables

This is a timetable for the 54 bus which goes from Rose Bay to Hillhead.

Rose Bay	0905	1005	1105	1205	1305	1405
Bourne	0925	1025	–	–	1325	1425
Troy	1015	1115	–	–	1415	1515
Kirby	1030	–	1210	–	1430	1530
Cox Green	1055	–	1235	–	–	1555
Hillhead	1135	1220	1315	1355	1530	1635

example

If I catch the first bus of the day how long will it take me to go to Hillhead?

- Use a time line to help you answer this question.
- Plot out each answer and use the timeline to help you to answer the next 5 questions.

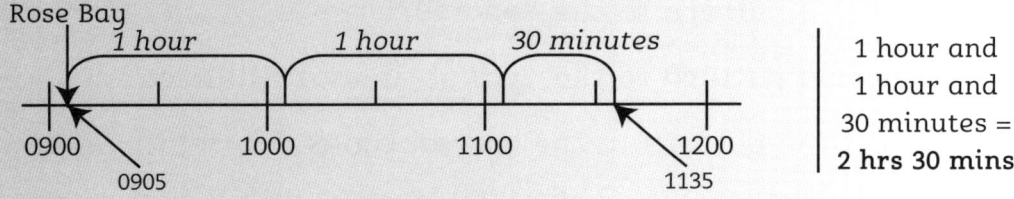

1 hour and
1 hour and
30 minutes =
2 hrs 30 mins

- **Now answer the next 5 questions.**

1   How long does the 1305 bus from Rose Bay take to travel to Hillhead?

2   How long does the 0925 bus from Bourne take to get to Cox Green?

3   I have just missed the 1025 bus from Bourne. How long do I have to wait until the next bus?

4   I get on the bus at Kirby at 1530 and get off at Cox Green at 1555. How long was I on the bus?

5   Work out the difference in journey time between the fastest and the slowest bus.

2

Name: _____ Date: _____

TARGET

I can use a timeline to help work out the difference between two times in a timetable.

☐ ☐ ☐ ☐

4

Name: _____ Date: _____

TARGET

I can compare information that is presented on a timetable.

☐ ☐ ☐ ☐

1

Name: _____ Date: _____

TARGET

I can use a timeline to work out the difference in time from the beginning of an event to its end.

☐ ☐ ☐ ☐

3

Name: _____ Date: _____

TARGET

I can extract information from timetables to answer questions.

☐ ☐ ☐ ☐

Revision and Examinations

What is the problem? Many students protest that it is impossible to revise maths – they cannot draw mind-maps or get someone to test them on their recollection. Maths does not lend itself to making notes or working with a friend.

Where to start: Maths is, in fact, quite easy to revise – but it is time-consuming, because the student must practise all the techniques up to the point of automaticity. **The best time to start revision is at the beginning of the course.** If a student makes *personal*, *meaningful* notes that remind him of what he did to complete each task, he can use them later to make sense of half-forgotten techniques. If he records examples with his own comments, he can go over them as he tries to do similar tasks. If he writes down some similar questions, they will be handy for him to use for practice.

For example:

Front

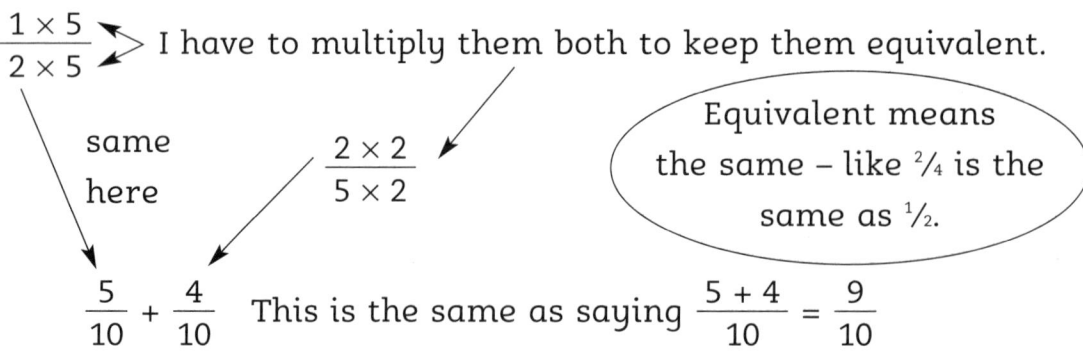

Revision card

Adding fractions

$\frac{1}{2} + \frac{2}{5}$

Remember!
Fractions must be the same size pieces

The smallest number in both the 2× and 5× table is 10.

$\frac{1 \times 5}{2 \times 5}$ → I have to multiply them both to keep them equivalent.

same here

$\frac{2 \times 2}{5 \times 2}$

Equivalent means the same – like ²/₄ is the same as ½.

$\frac{5}{10} + \frac{4}{10}$ This is the same as saying $\frac{5 + 4}{10} = \frac{9}{10}$

On the **Back** of the cards, write some practice questions, e.g. ¹/₃ + ³/₄ =

- **Repeated review leads to improved recollection**

To ensure good recall, a student needs to go over a skill half a dozen times or more – and that is once he has a reasonable understanding of what he is doing.

Transferring learning to long-term memory:

Developing a pattern of regular review boosts learning.

20%	40%	60%	80%	100%	100%
Learning – no review	Review after 24 hours	Review after 48 hours	Review after one week	Review after one month	Review before exams

The revision graph shows that, if a student does not review learning within 24 hours, his recall will drop to 20%. This can be doubled if he goes over what he has learnt – and, if he reviews again the next day, recall can rise to 60%. Insert another revision session a week later and he will remember in the region of 80% of the material. A final review a month later will ensure that he remembers nearly all of the content. (Jenny Cogan and Mary Flecker: (2004) *Dyslexia in the Secondary School*. The study strategy detailed on page 7 can help a student organise his learning to fit this pattern.

- Making the best use of revision time.

Tony Buzan in his book *Use Your Head (2003, BBC Books, ISBN 0563488999)* shows how students' learning declines if they try to study for too long at a time. They remember best what they have studied at the *beginning* of a revision session and what they went over *most recently*.

Students can help themselves by making revision sessions short and frequent so that they have a lot of beginnings and endings. Sessions should be no longer that 30 – 45 minutes, before the student takes a break, has a little exercise and a drink of water. He should try to avoid drinks containing caffeine, which creates highs and lows.

Revision session

How to maximise learning:

Spend 5 minutes working out a sample question on your last topic.	Take 20 – 30 minutes going over your new topic.	Close your books and spend 5 minutes testing yourself to see how much you recall.

After a short break, repeat the pattern.

Spend 5 minutes working out a sample question on your last topic.	Take 20 – 30 minutes going over your new topic.	Close your books and spend 5 minutes testing yourself to see how much you recall.

The student has now studied the topic and tested himself twice on his recall. If he finds he is remembering it well, he can put it aside until a later session, but if he has not retained it, he knows that he must study it further, or ask for help.

Covering the topics

Often students feel overwhelmed by the sheer amount of revision they have to cover. They do not know where to start or how to plan their time.

Teachers should help jump start the process by working out a detailed revision plan with them, including topic breakdowns.

Small bite-sized sub topics can be covered in a single revision session, and as a student ticks them off, he is left feeling that he has achieved something.

Topic Breakdown

You should be able to cover each segment in fifteen minutes.

Tick each sub-topic off when you have worked on it and completed a question successfully.

This will ensure that you are giving each topic enough time and not missing any out.

Date revised				
Percentages:				
Find 10% no calculator	✓	✓		
Find other percentages	✓			
Use calculator for %				
Percentage change				
Finding original price				

- Remember you can learn what you don't understand, but you cannot apply it.

You need to use **VARIOUS** methods of revision to make use of your best learning style.

Visualise – use posters and diagrams. Add colour. Practise seeing visual images. Link pictures with learning. Use memory pegs to link information in a way that is memorable.

Associate – make connections between target information. Remember things because they are part of a pattern, or because they remind you of something else.

Repeat – go over information. Break it down into small achievable chunks and make sure you have time to go over each section several times. Verbalise what you are doing and practise skills.

Interest – do try different ways of learning. Practise on questions, teach skills to others, play games, use computer programs, reward yourself for completing work sessions.

Organise – make sure you have a revision plan. Break down topics into small segments and tick off subjects covered. Make your revision sessions short – you remember best what you do at the beginning and the end of a session, so give yourself plenty of beginnings and endings.

Understand – if you do not understand a topic, get help! Go to a friend and get him to teach you. Go to your teacher and ask for advice. Give yourself enough time to make sense of your topics.

Share – you do not have to do it on your own. Some of the most successful revision is done in the company of friends. Teach a topic to another, discuss how to carry out tasks. Play games. Work together.

Using examination questions to revise

It is worth pointing out that *the student does not need to know everything*. The object of taking an examination is to get the best possible grade. **This can be achieved better by getting right the things he can do than by struggling to learn every element he does not understand**.

Break each topic down into smaller parts, so that a student can feel **successful** in studying the earlier elements of a topic, rather than feeling he has failed in understanding the whole topic. If reviewing percentages, for example, he will see that he can carry out the first three tasks without difficulty and that he can remember what to do for the fourth – it is only one sub-topic that he finds really difficult. **Build success into revision**.

Some students do better in exams than expected, because they know how to work the system. One way of improving students' success in exams is to use vast quantities of **past questions** and past papers to practise and practise the skills needed. Show them the pattern of questions and they will begin to recognise types of question and know how to tackle them, which will reduce their anxiety.

There is often a lot of information packed into an apparently simple question and a student must first be able to **read** the question. To do this, he needs to separate it into chunks, using the punctuation to help him make sense of it, before breaking it down into small tasks. He needs to be able to add, subtract, multiply and divide. He needs to have a grasp of the basics of working with percentages, averages, substituting numbers for letters, angles, area, volume and reading and completing graphs.

When first working on examination-style questions, it can be useful to go through them, showing students how to go through their **PACES** to analyse them and decide what the question is testing and then state what they would need to do to find the answer. Next they can estimate an answer before finally answering the question, **knowing what they have to do.**

Past papers

- Extract and use genuine questions from past papers from the beginning of the course, so that students can get accustomed to the way questions are asked.
- Build up a bank of topic-specific question of slowly increasing difficulty.
- Go through the target questions with students. Break down the question and discuss what needs to be done.
- It does not matter if you re-use the same questions – familiarity develops confidence.
- Start with questions that are well within a student's capability – once he loses confidence, his ability to carry out any tasks will be reduced.
- Keep the amount of work to be done small enough for the student to take his time.

In examinations themselves, students will do better if they

- Read the instructions more than once
- At the beginning of the exam:
  draw up a tables square and
  write down all the formulae they can remember
- Analyse each question and note down what it is testing
- Note down the processes they must use
- Estimate a likely answer
- Solve the problem
- Check the answer
- Omit and come back to questions they find difficult
- Use practical tools, such as number lines, as necessary.

Students say, 'I can do maths in class, but in exams I forget what I am supposed to be doing'.

The variety of topics on the paper causes most problems. Before a student can answer a question he has to decide what he is being asked to do. What can he do to help himself?

- Keep calm. Massaging behind the ears can help to reduce panic. So can rhythmic breathing exercises
- Read each question twice – then read it again and sub-vocalise while thinking about what it is asking him to do
- Highlight key words and figures
- First answer the questions he thinks he can do
- Go through his PACES
- Work slowly – most people lose marks on things *they can easily get right*, like adding figures
- Check he has answered the question
- Decide which questions to ignore
- Proof read his work to be sure it says what he means it to say
- Keep an eye on the time. In maths, he cannot simply divide the time equally between the number of questions. The later part of the paper contains the higher level questions that will probably take longer. But the student should give himself time markers. Find the half-way question and aim to reach it before the half-way point of the exam. Plan to leave fifteen minutes at the end of the paper to check over answers.
- If he has been given extra time, the student needs to know how much longer he will have and when he will finish. Many students feel the chief advantage of extra time is the opportunity to read the questions through more slowly to be sure of understanding them and to be able to check work at the end of the exam.

TARGET 1

Name: _____ Date: _____

I have made a revision plan that identifies topics to cover.

☐ ☐ ☐ ☐

TARGET 2

Name: _____ Date: _____

I am in the process of building up a resource of revision cards with examples and useful notes.

☐ ☐ ☐ ☐

TARGET 3

Name: _____ Date: _____

I have identified areas of weakness and asked my teacher to help me.

☐ ☐ ☐ ☐

TARGET 4

Name: _____ Date: _____

I am able to identify what the questions expect me to do and complete practice papers.

☐ ☐ ☐ ☐

Answers to Photocopiable Sheets

Skills Area 1

What questions mean (1.1, page 16)
1. a) +   b) ×
   c) –   d) + and –
2. ÷
3. ÷
4. –
5. ÷
6. ×

What questions mean (1.2, page 17)
1. + ÷ and ×
2. +
3. a) ÷ b) ×
4. + and –
5. + and – , or – and –
6. –
7. ×

Roughly what is the answer? (1.3, page 37, 38)
1. +   500 + 200 = 700   706
2. +   400 + 60 = 460   453
3. –   700 – 300 = 400   378
4. ×   20 × 100 = 2000   2352
5. ÷   6000 ÷ 30 = 200   207.41
6. ÷   2000 ÷ 4 = 500   £498.50
7. × and +   3 × 2 + 3 = 9   £8.96
8. ×   2 × 50 = 100 $96.53
9. ÷   300 ÷ 50 = 6   6½ hours

Roughly what is the answer? (1.4, page 39, 40)
1. ÷   3000 ÷ 30 = 100   108
2. ×   40 × 10 = 400   £370.50
3. +   90 + 40 + 30 = 160   £158.02
4. + and –   40 + 60 + 10 = 110, 150 – 110 = 40
   £35.67
5. ×   10 × 8 = 80   78.3173
6. –   8000 – 1000 = 7000   £6420
7. ÷   4000 ÷ 20 = 200   185.476
8. ×   20 × 3 = 60   56

Skills Area 2

Adding and subtracting 9 and 11 (2.1a, page 48)
Adding 9
1. 23   2. 32   3. 48   4. 61
5. 87   6. 91   7. 56

Subtracting 9
1. 14   2. 22   3. 59   4. 47
5. 30   6. 83   7. 67

Adding 11
1. 34   2. 28   3. 48   4. 63
5. 89   6. 74   7. 91

Subtracting 11
1. 26   2. 33   3. 40   4. 88
5. 49   6. 41   7. 18

Adding and subtracting 9 and 11 (2.1b, page 49)
Adding 9
1. 32   2. 42   3. 48   4. 75
5. 82   6. 94   7. 56

Subtracting 9
1. 22   2. 36   3. 74   4. 43
5. 86   6. 39   7. 58

Adding 11
1. 58   2. 44   3. 68   4. 84
5. 52   6. 74   7. 99

Subtracting 11
1. 36   2. 22   3. 47   4. 82
5. 53   6. 14   7. 28

Multiplying and dividing by 10 and 100 (2.2, page 52)
Multiplying by 10
1. 230   2. 330   3. 39   4. 667.5
5. 734   6. 852.5   7. 472

Multiplying by 100
1. 3100   2. 4500   3. 830   4. 5245
5. 950   6. 480   7. 6775

Dividing by 10 (page 52)

1. 4.7   2. 3.3   3. 57.2   4. 73.1
5. 410.3   6. 6.35   7. 8.872

Dividing by 100

1. 4.71   2. 3.324   3. 0.58   4. 0.93
5. 0.0684   6. 0.0025   7. 0.03905

Using a hundred square (2.3, page 57)

1. 57   2. 94   3. 90   4. 54
5. 62   6. 79

7.

+	53	25	15	47	61
9	62	34	24	56	70
14	67	39	29	61	75
21	74	46	36	68	82
5	58	30	20	52	66
35	88	60	50	82	96

8.

−	65	82	39	97	53
8	57	74	31	89	45
16	49	66	23	81	37
24	41	58	15	73	29
33	32	49	6	64	20
12	53	70	27	85	41

Using the tables square (2.4, page 61)

2. a) 28   b) 16   c) 54   d) 21
   e) 15   f) 10   g) 16   h) 42
   i) 16   j) 49   k) 18   l) 64
3. a) 9   b) 9   c) 8   d) 8
   e) 9   f) 10   g) 7   h) 7
   i) 9   j) 7   k) 9   l) 10
4. a) $9\frac{1}{4}$ b) $9\frac{1}{2}$ c) $5\frac{3}{5}$ d) $9\frac{6}{7}$
   e) $6\frac{5}{6}$ f) $7\frac{2}{3}$ g) $3\frac{5}{8}$ h) $2\frac{3}{10}$
   i) $3\frac{4}{9}$
5. 9
6. £63.

Key skills – addition and subtraction (2.5, page 68)

1. a) 907   b) 1831   c) 11235
2. 850
3. £35.38
4. a) 381   b) 371   c) 176
5. 775
6. £7.15
7. a) 307.96   b) 753.7163   c) 4705.52
   d) 2112.27   e) 118.35   f) 7887.82
8. a) 881   b) 1061   c) 735.2   d) 322.05
   e) 305.625   f) 623.25   g) 289.21   h) 2.125

Key skills – multiplication and division (2.6, page 69)

1. a) 7296   b) 19818   c) 8652
2. £493.75
3. £573.60
4. a) 19   b) 48   c) 624
5. £29255
6. £52.50
7. £114
8. 63.

Finding 10% and 1% (2.7, page 73)

1. 18   6. £845
2. 37.5 g   7. 3.42
3. 452.5 km   8. 2.5
4. £6.25   9. 8
5. £256.50   10. a) 150   b) 15

Finding awkward percentages (2.8, page 74)

1. a) 12   b) 24
2. a) £4.60   b) £2.30
3. a) $38   b) $57
4. 260
5. 2600
6. £799
7. £23.50
8. £7000
9. £138,000
10. £15.60

Using your calculator (2.9, page 79)

1. 6505.72   7. 20
2. 23.71   8. 34
3. £638   9. $10\frac{1}{6}$
4. £135784   10. $6\frac{11}{24}$
5. 25   11. $29\frac{1}{6}$
6. 169   12. $2\frac{22}{39}$

Using your calculator (2.10, page 80)

1. a) $(25 + 5) \div 10 - 6$ b) $25 + 5 \div (10 - 6)$
   c) $25 + (5 \div 10) - 6$
2. $(25 + 5) \div (10 - 6)$

3. a) $\dfrac{40 + 300}{22.8 \times 4.9} = \dfrac{340}{100} = 3.4$

   b) $\dfrac{40 + 300}{22.8 \times 4.9} = 2.952$

4. 153.93804 cm²   6. 46.02433237 cm
5. 452.3893421 m²   7. 62.83185307 m

Working with money (2.11, page 84)

1.
2×73	1.46
4×42	1.68
$26 \div 2$	0.13
1.5×1.24	1.86
$3.80 \div 4$	0.95
	6.08

   $20.00 - 6.08 = £13.92$

2. $£15.50 \times 23 = £356.50$

   $£356.50 - £207 = £149.50.$

3. $£21322.14$

Working with money (2.12, page 85)

1.

Value of coin	Number of coins	Value × number of coins	Sub-total
£2	3	2×3	£6.00
£1	7	1×7	£7.00
50p	13	0.50×13	£6.50
20p	52	0.20×52	£10.40
10p	26	0.10×26	£2.60
5p	44	0.05×44	£2.20
2p	124	0.02×124	£2.48
1p	68	0.01×68	£0.68
	Total		£37.86

2. £37.58 to the nearest penny

   35

3. £12.48

   £16.80

Using and converting measurements 1 (2.13, page 89, 90)

1.

Imperial measures		
12 inches	=	1 foot
3 feet	=	1 yard
1760 yards	=	1 mile
20 fluid ounces	=	1 pint
8 pints	=	1 gallon
16 ounces	=	1 pound
14 pounds	=	1 stone
8 stone	=	1 hundredweight
20 hundredweight	=	1 ton

2. 36 inches = 3 feet

3. 7 pounds = half a stone

4.

Metric measures		
10 millimetres	=	1 centimetre
100 centimetres	=	1 metre
1000 millimetres	=	1 metre
1000 metres	=	1 kilometre
100 centilitres	=	1 litre
1000 millilitres	=	1 litre
1000 milligrams	=	1 gram
1000 grams	=	1 kilogram
1000 kilograms	=	1 tonne

5. $1000 \times 5 = 5000$ metres

6. $1000 \times 1000 = 1000,000$ grams in a tonne

Using and converting measurements 2 (2.14, page 91)

1.

Imperial		Metric
1 inch	≈	2.5 centimetres
1 foot	≈	30 centimetres
5 miles	≈	8 kilometres
1 mile	≈	1.6 kilometres
1.75 pints	≈	1 litre
1 gallon	≈	4.5 litres
2.2 pounds	≈	1 kilogram

2. $16 \times 14 \times 5 = 1120$ ounces

3. $1760 \times 3 = 5280$ yards

4. $2.5 \times 19 = 25$ centimetres

5. $270 \div 2.5 = 108$ inches

6. $7 \times 4.5 = 31.5$ litres

7. $17.6 \div 2.2 = 8$ kg

8. $157 \div 2.5 = 63$ inches

9. $540 \times 4.5 = 2430$ litres

10. $85 \times 1.6 = 136$ km

Finding the time (2.15, page 97)

Box 1: a) 2 hours

        b) 2 hours

        c) 6 hours

Box 2: a) 55 minutes

        b) 40 minutes

        c) 45 minutes

Box 3: a) 1 hour 20 minutes

        b) 1 hour 30 minutes

        c) 1 hour 45 minutes

Box 4: a) 30 minutes

        b) 1 hour 5 minutes

        c) 45 minutes

Box 5: a) 2 hours
        b) 1 hour 30 minutes
        c) 1 hour 45 minutes

Skills Area 3

Understanding questions (3.1, page 105) actual answers

1. a) c to the power of five
   b) $5n + 4p$
2. a) $4t + 6 = 3t + 11$
      $4t - 3t = 11 - 6$
      $t = 5$
   b) $3(2d - 5) = 9$
      $2d - 5 = 9 \div 3$
      $2d = 3 + 5$
      $d = 8 \div 2$
      $d = 4$
3. $4.5 \times 2 \times 3 = 27 \text{ m}^3$
4. Any pattern where the edges all meet.
5. £2400
6. a) 0.375   b) 37.5%   c) £350

Understanding questions (3.2, page 106) actual answers

1. 60
2. $2b(b - 5) + b(b + 2)$
   $2b^2 - 10b + b^2 + 2b$
   $3b^2 - 8b$
3. It is an isosceles triangle.
   ACB and ABC are equal, so $180 - 50 = 130$.
   Half 130 is 65
4. There are 20 counters. 5 are blue. There is a $^5/_{20}$ chance of picking a blue counter. $^5/_{20}$ is the same as $^1/_4$
   There are 20 counters. Only 2 are green. There is a $^{18}/_{20}$ chance of picking a counter that is not green. $^{18}/_{20}$ is the same as $^9/_{10}$.
5. a) median = 3
   b) mode = 3
   c) mean = 2.65

Finding percentages (3.3, page 114)

1. a) 8.9   b) 121   c) 98   d) 123.48
2. 90%
3. 90%
4. 95%, 65%, 75%
5. 600%

6. 30%
7. £500
8. £600

Finding the average (3.4, page 118)

1. mode = 3
   median = 3
   mean = 3.4166
   range = 8
2. mean = 12
   mode = 14
   median = 13.5
   the mode is highest

Less than nothing (3.5, page 122)

1. 20
2. 11
3. 11
4. a) 2   b) –10   c) –4   d) –7
   e) 5   f) –4
5. 18 , 9 , 15 , 15
6. a) 12   b) –12   c) 12   d) –12
   e) 3   f) –3   g) –3   h) 3
   i) –3   j) 3   k) 40   l) –40

Working with ratio (3.6, page 126)

1. £60
2. 180g
3. a) 4:5:1   b) 1:5:2   c) 5:7:3   d) 1:4:2
   e) 3:8:6   f) 3:2:4
4. £100.
   There is £240 altogether.

Working with fractions (3.7, page 132)

1. You need to make both sides into twelfths.
$$\frac{1}{4} + \frac{1}{3} = \frac{3}{12} + \frac{4}{12} = \frac{7}{12}$$

2. $\frac{1}{2} = \frac{2}{4}$ so $\frac{2}{4} + \frac{1}{4} = \frac{3}{4}$

3. There are 8 pieces visible
$\frac{1}{4} = \frac{2}{8}$ add $\frac{1}{8}$ so

$$\frac{2 + 1}{8} = \frac{3}{8}$$

Working with fractions (3.8, page 133)

1. $\dfrac{1}{4} = \dfrac{2}{8} = \dfrac{3}{12} = \dfrac{4}{16} = \dfrac{5}{20} = \dfrac{6}{24} = \dfrac{25}{100}$

   $\dfrac{1}{2} = \dfrac{3}{6} = \dfrac{4}{8} = \dfrac{7}{14} = \dfrac{9}{18} = \dfrac{12}{24}$

   $\dfrac{2}{6} = \dfrac{3}{9} = \dfrac{4}{12} = \dfrac{5}{15}$

2. 0.75   75%
3. 0.875   87.5%
4. 0.35 $\dfrac{7}{20}$

5. a) $\dfrac{3}{4}$ b) $\dfrac{11}{15}$

   c) $\dfrac{5}{12}$ d) $\dfrac{11}{40}$

6. a) $\dfrac{1}{3}$ b) $\dfrac{3}{5}$

   c) $1\frac{1}{2}$ d) $\dfrac{5}{6}$

Working with letters (3.9, page 140)

1. a) $4a$ b) $3a + b$
   c) $2s + 3t - v$ d) $5m + p$
2. a) $4ab$ b) $5gh$
   c) bdn d) $5cd$
3. a) 9   b) 2
   c) 7   d) 45
4. a) 11   b) 13   c) 4
   d) 30   e) 6   f) 34
5. a) $x = 3$ b) $x = 2$
   c) $x = 5$ d) $x = 5$

Working with letters (3.10, page 141)

1. a) $x = 3$ b) $x = 1$
   c) $x = 2.5$ d) $x = 3$
2. $C = 25\,g + 100$
   Tom and Mia's reception will cost
   $C = 25 \times 45 + 100 = £1225$
3. $E = 200 + 70$
   If Kelly worked 10 hours overtime she
   earned $200 + (7 \times 10) = £270$
   If she earned £249, she received

249 – 200 = £49 for overtime.
49 ÷ 7 shows that she worked 7 hours
overtime.

Working with area (3.11, page 156)

1. 15 m²
2. 40 cm²
3. 25 m²
4. triangle = $\frac{1}{2}bh$
   circle = πr^2
   rectangle = bh
   trapezium = $\frac{1}{2}(a + b)h$
   parallelogram = bh

Working with volume (3.12, page 157)

1. One layer = lb = 50 cm²
   Four layers = lbh = 200 cm²
2. 785 cm²
   This is a cylinder
   To find the volume, I must find the area of
   the end and multiply it by the length.
   $V = \pi r^2 l$
3. A prism is a three-dimensional shape that
   is exactly the same all along its length.
   If I find the area of the cross-section and
   multiply it by the length, it gives the
   volume.

Reading timetables (3.14, page 169)

1. Rose Bay
2. Five
3. Hillhead
4. Six
5. It leaves at hourly intervals
6. No.
7. It stops in a different number of places.
8. The 12.05. It stops at the fewest places.
9. The 09.05 and the 14.05.
10. Three.
11. The 12.05.
12. 13.05.
13. The 14.05

Calculating with timetables (3.15, page 170)

1. 2 hours 25 minutes
2. 1 hour 30 minutes
3. 3 hours
4. 25 minutes
5. 40 minutes

Resource Sheets

Using the Resource Sheets

Resource sheets 1 – place value

Sheet 1a

- Stick a see-through strip over the decimal point column.
- Use strips of paper marked in columns.
- Write numbers on the strips and ask students to multiply or divide by 10, 100 or 1000 to see how the number changes.

Sheet 1b and 1c

- Use with money or other concrete objects to illustrate place value and exchange. Sheet 1c extends hundreds, tens and units to larger numbers.

Sheet 1d

- Use with money – whole pounds and pence – or other concrete objects to illustrate place value and exchange with numbers bigger and smaller than one whole unit.

Resource sheets 2 – number bond triangles

Sheets 2a and 2b

- Large triangles can be used to illustrate number bonds, as on page 23.
- Smaller triangle sheets can be used to build up confidence in recognising the way numbers relate to each other.

Resource sheet 3 – hundred squares

- Hundred squares can be used for building confidence in number relationships and for adding and subtracting (page 54 and 55)
- Visualising the hundred square develops confidence with mental strategies for adding and subtracting 9 and 11.

Resource sheet 4 – times table squares

- Use times table square with square numbers until the student increases in confidence.
- Then build regular completion of tables squares into lessons.

Resource sheets 5 – timelines

Sheet 5a
- This sheet relates the different ways of expressing time. A student should manufacture his own timeline, or have a photocopy available.

Sheet 5b and 5c
- These can be used to help work out the passage of time. They can be enlarged. If covered with sticky-backed plastic, the student can re-use this repeatedly to work out the passage of time.

Resource sheet 6 – fraction strips
- Fraction strips offer a visual and physical way of seeing and understanding the difference between fraction sizes and how they relate to whole numbers.
- They offer an opportunity to see and understand equivalence.
- They provide a student with a way of seeing how fractions can be made the same size to be added or subtracted.

Resource sheet 7 – 1cm squared paper
- Many students with weaknesses in maths find the size of square in standard maths exercise books to be too small.
- 1cm paper enables them to place a single numeral in each square and to keep their figures in line – which helps them to reach the right answer.

Resource sheets 8, 9 and 10 – VARIOUS, STUD and PACES
- These provide A4 sheets of the three strategies referred to throughout the text.
- They can be enlarged to use as posters or reduced to give a student a memory card on the strategy.

Resource sheet 11 – angle dial
- This is used in conjunction with the tasks on page 145 and page 146 to help students work with angles.
- It is also useful for students working on pie charts.

Resource sheets 12 – shape reference cards
- The Fact sheets are examples of how a student can build up a resource bank of information about different shapes (page 147).
- They can be extended to cover other two-dimensional and three-dimensional shapes.

Resource sheet 13 – amount cards
- These can be used to build confidence with place value (page 25).

Resource sheet 14 – scales
- These should be used to read quantities from different scales (page 160).

Place value

Photocopiable
resource sheet 1a

hundreds	tens	units	decimal point	1/10	1/100	1/1000
			•			
			•			
			•			
			•			
			•			
			•			
			•			
			•			
			•			

Place value chart

units	tens	hundreds

Place value chart

millions			thousands			hundreds		
H	T	U	H	T	U	H	T	U

hundreds	tens	units	$\bullet$	tenths $\dfrac{1}{10}$	hundredths $\dfrac{1}{100}$

Number bond triangles

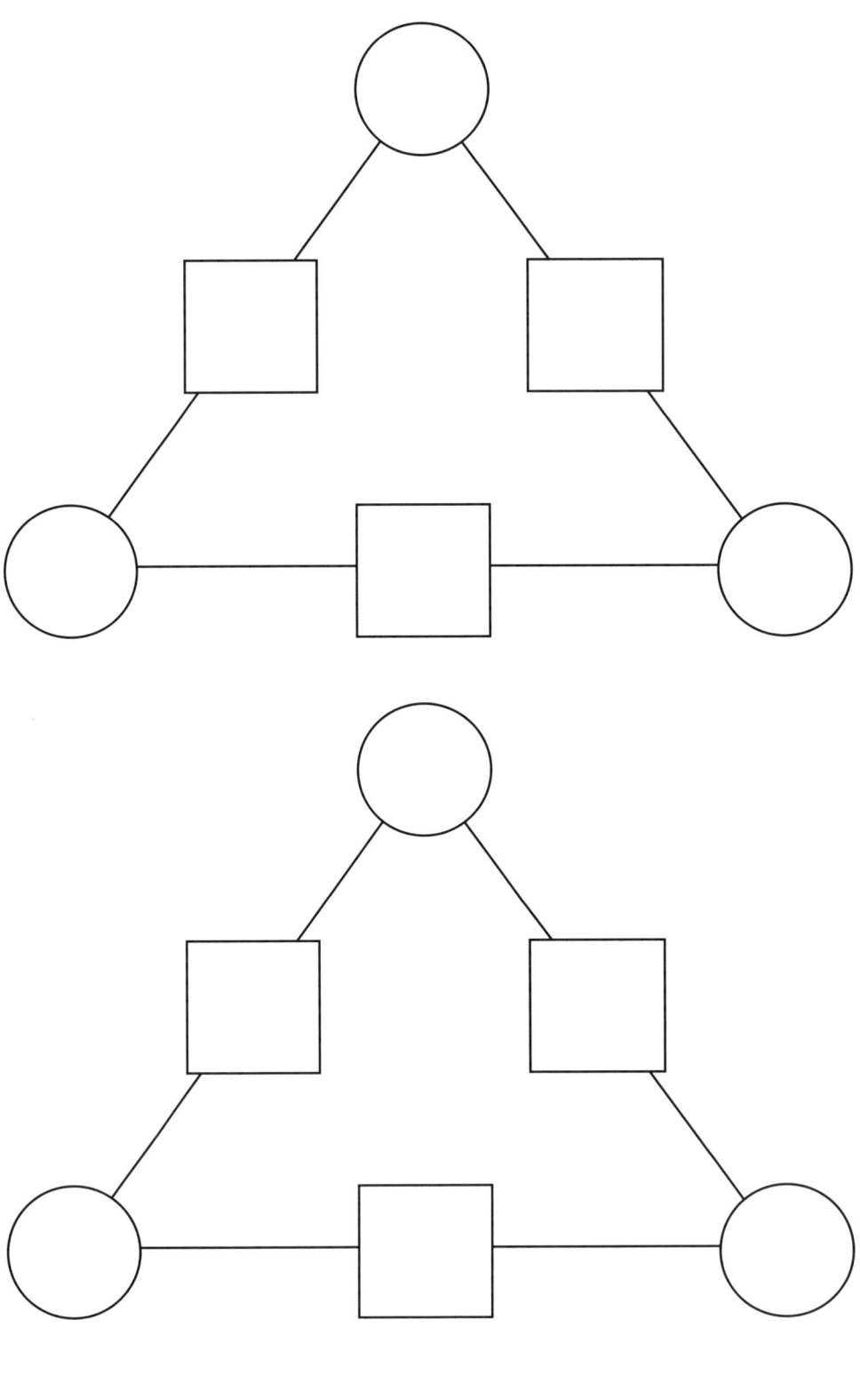

Number triangles

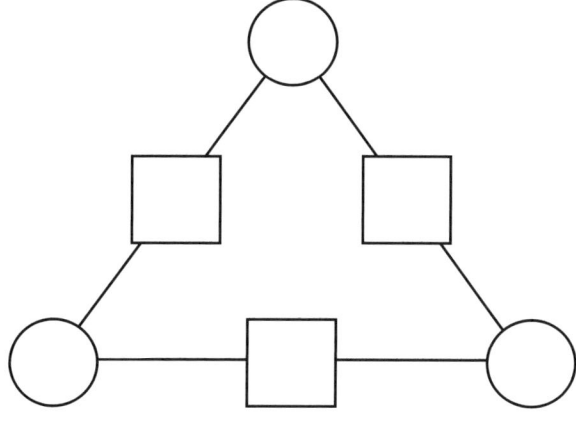

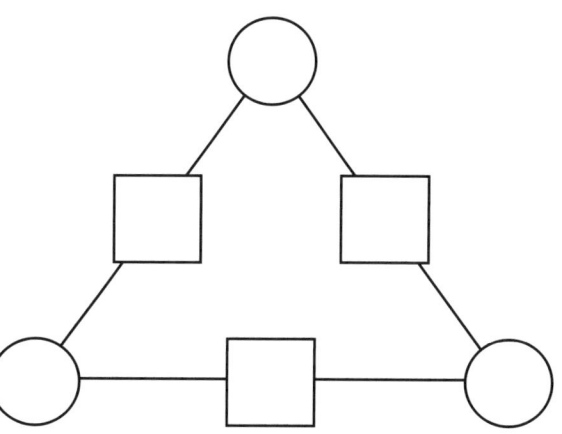

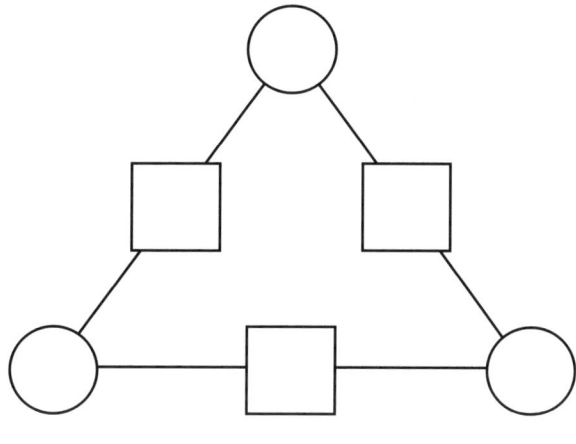

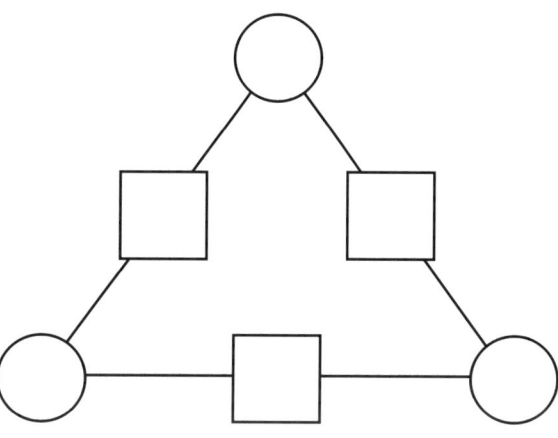

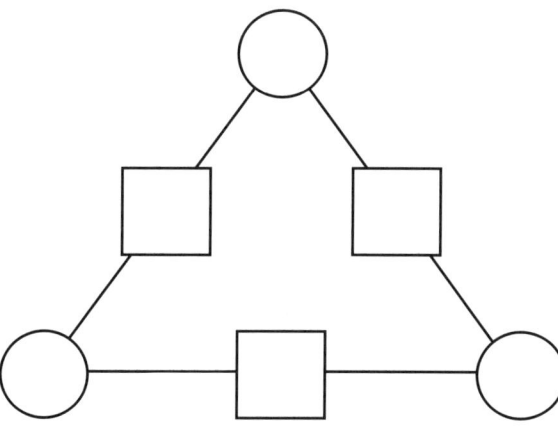

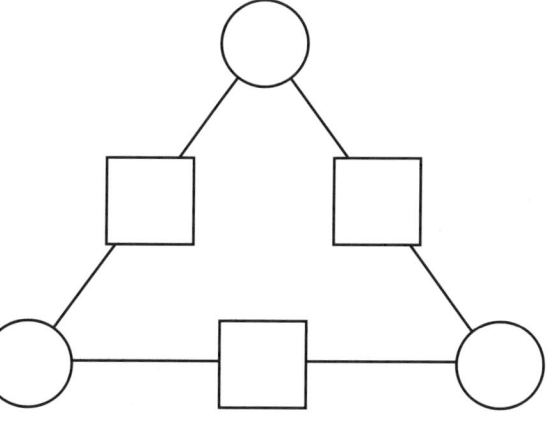

Hundred squares

0	1	2	3	4	5	6	7	8	9
10	11	12	13	14	15	16	17	18	19
20	21	22	23	24	25	26	27	28	29
30	31	32	33	34	35	36	37	38	39
40	41	42	43	44	45	46	47	48	49
50	51	52	53	54	55	56	57	58	59
60	61	62	63	64	65	66	67	68	69
70	71	72	73	74	75	76	77	78	79
80	81	82	83	84	85	86	87	88	89
90	91	92	93	94	95	96	97	98	99

1	2	3	4	5	6	7	8	9	10
11	12	13	14	15	16	17	18	19	20
21	22	23	24	25	26	27	28	29	30
31	32	33	34	35	36	37	38	39	40
41	42	43	44	45	46	47	48	49	50
51	52	53	54	55	56	57	58	59	60
61	62	63	64	65	66	67	68	69	70
71	72	73	74	75	76	77	78	79	80
81	82	83	84	85	86	87	88	89	90
91	92	93	94	95	96	97	98	99	100

Times table squares

×	0	1	2	3	4	5	6	7	8	9	10
0	0	0	0	0	0	0	0	0	0	0	0
1	0	1	2	3	4	5	6	7	8	9	10
2	0	2	4	6	8	10	12	14	16	18	20
3	0	3	6	9	12	15	18	21	24	27	30
4	0	4	8	12	16	20	24	28	32	36	40
5	0	5	10	15	20	25	30	35	40	45	50
6	0	6	12	18	24	30	36				60
7	0	7	14	21	28	35		49	56		70
8	0	8	16	24	32	40		56	64		80
9	0	9	18	27	36	45				81	90
10	0	10	20	30	40	50	60	70	80	90	100

×											

24 hour clock

The new day starts at midnight

Analogue	Digital	24 hour
1 o'clock	1:00am	0100
2 o'clock	2:00am	0200
3 o'clock	3:00am	0300
4 o'clock	4:00am	0400
5 o'clock	5:00am	0500
6 o'clock	6:00am	0600
7 o'clock	7:00am	0700
8 o'clock	8:00am	0800
9 o'clock	9:00am	0900
10 o'clock	10:00am	1000
11 o'clock	11:00am	1100
12 o'clock	12:00	1200
1 o'clock	1:00pm	1300
2 o'clock	2:00pm	1400
3 o'clock	3:00pm	1500
4 o'clock	4:00pm	1600
5 o'clock	5:00pm	1700
6 o'clock	6:00pm	1800
7 o'clock	7:00pm	1900
8 o'clock	8:00pm	2000
9 o'clock	9:00pm	2100
10 o'clock	10:00pm	2200
11 o'clock	11:00pm	2300
12 o'clock	12.00pm	0000

Making a timeline

Cut out the strips and enlarge if you want to. Stick them together to make a continuous row.

The beginning of the long strip is 12 o'clock, midnight, 0000.

Count off six divisions and mark in 1 o'clock, 1:00am, 0100.

Count off six divisions and mark in 2 o'clock, 2.00am, 0200.

Continue until you have a timeline as long as the strip allows.

Timeline

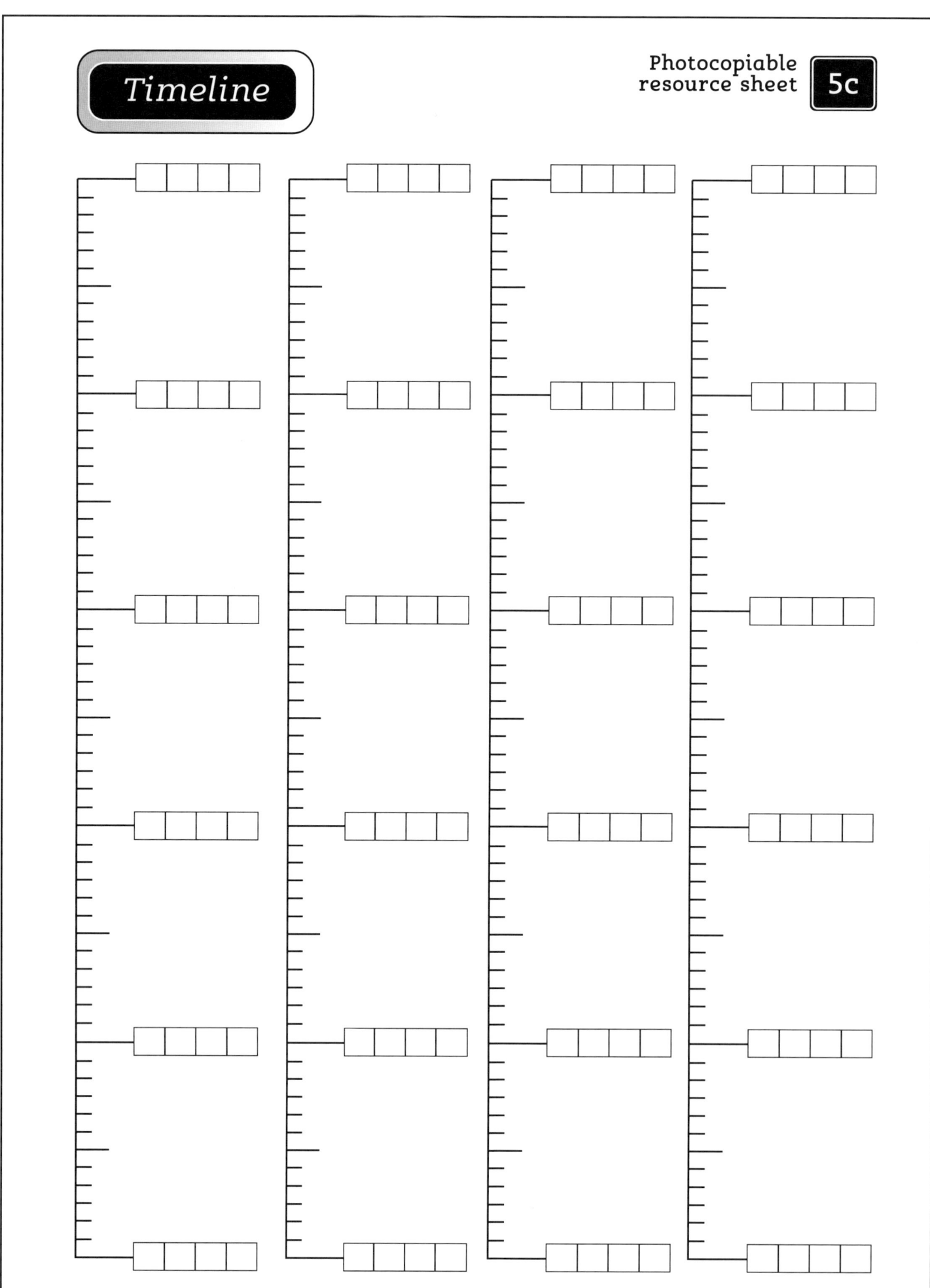

Fraction strips

1cm squared paper

Photocopiable resource sheet 7

 **Visualise** – make pictures in your head.

 **Associate** – link ideas and make connections.

 **Repeat** – go over learning again and again until it is solid.

 **Interest** – find ways to make learning fun.

 **Organise** – break topics down and plan your time.

 **Understand** – or you cannot learn! Get help, if necessary.

 **Share** – work with a friend. Teach and test each other.

 **See** – look at what you are studying. Make pictures in your head to make it connect.

 **Talk** – put into words what the task is asking you to do.

 **Understand** – make links between all the parts of the task and see how to get to the answer.

 **Do** – once the pattern is clear, carry out the task.

 **Picture** the question as a whole. What is the question about?

 **Analyse** the question. What steps do you need to take to complete the task?

 **Consider** what you have to do. How do you carry out each part of the task?

 **Estimate**. What sort of answer should you expect? Bigger? Smaller? Roughly how big?

 **Solve**. Now you are ready to work out the answer. Write your solution – and make **sure** you check for **silly** mistakes.

*Avoid making silly mistakes
in answering questions!*

Go through your PACES

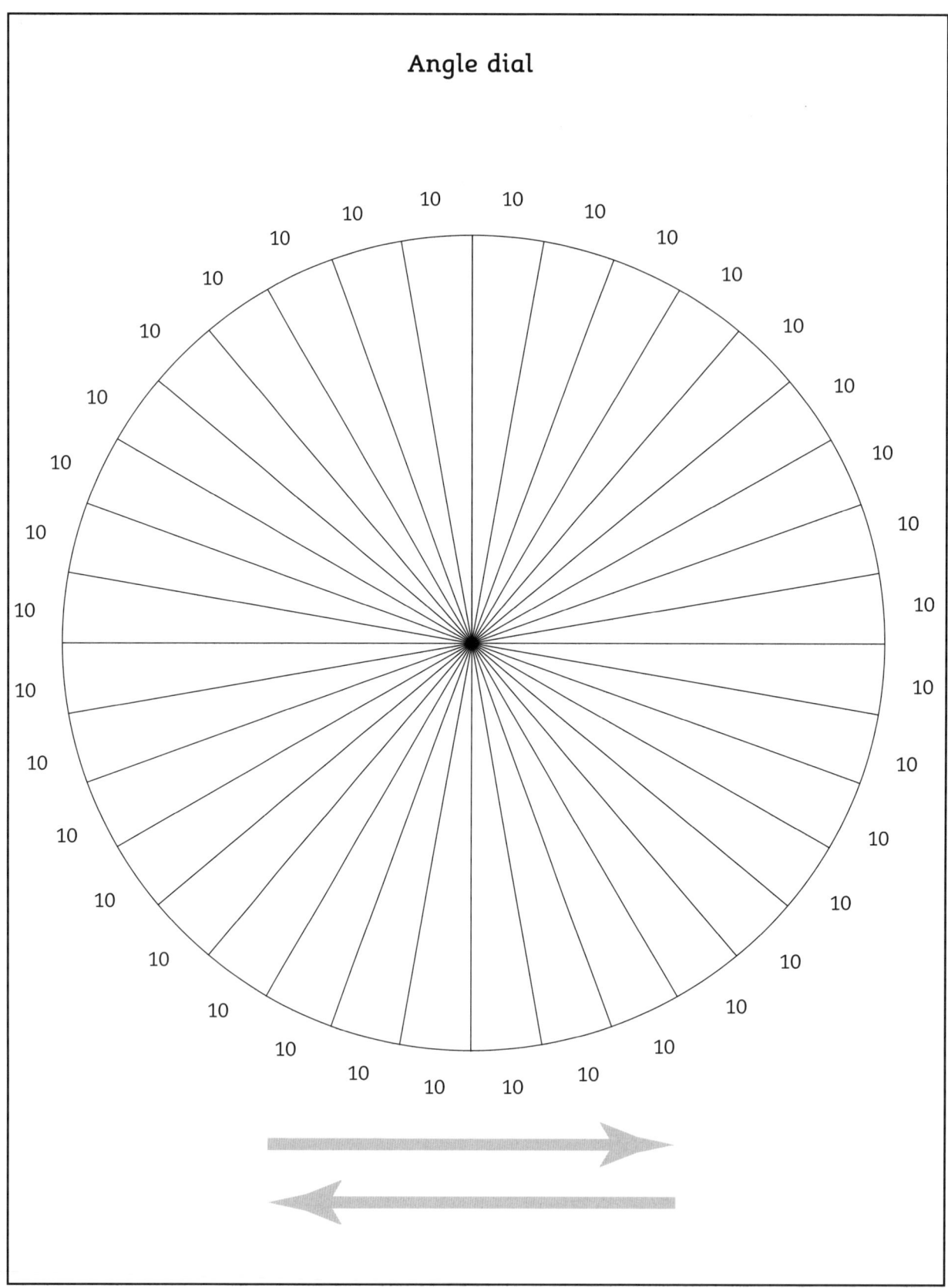

Angle dial

Angle dial

10 10 10 10 10 10 10 10 10 10 10 10 10 10 10 10 10 10 10 10 10 10 10 10 10 10 10 10 10 10 10 10 10 10 10 10

Triangle facts

Equilateral triangle
all sides equal
all angles equal (60°)

Area of a triangle
is found by multiplying
the *base* by the *height*
and *halving* the answer

$$A = \frac{bh}{2}$$

h

b

Isoceles triangle
two sides the same length
two angles equal

3 sides
angles add up to 180°

Right-angled triangle
one angle 90°

Longest side called
the hypotenuse

c

b

a

Scalene triangle
all sides different
all angles different

**Using a triangle to
rearrange the
formula for
Pythagoras**

$a^2 + b^2 = c^2$

c^2

−   −

a^2 + b^2

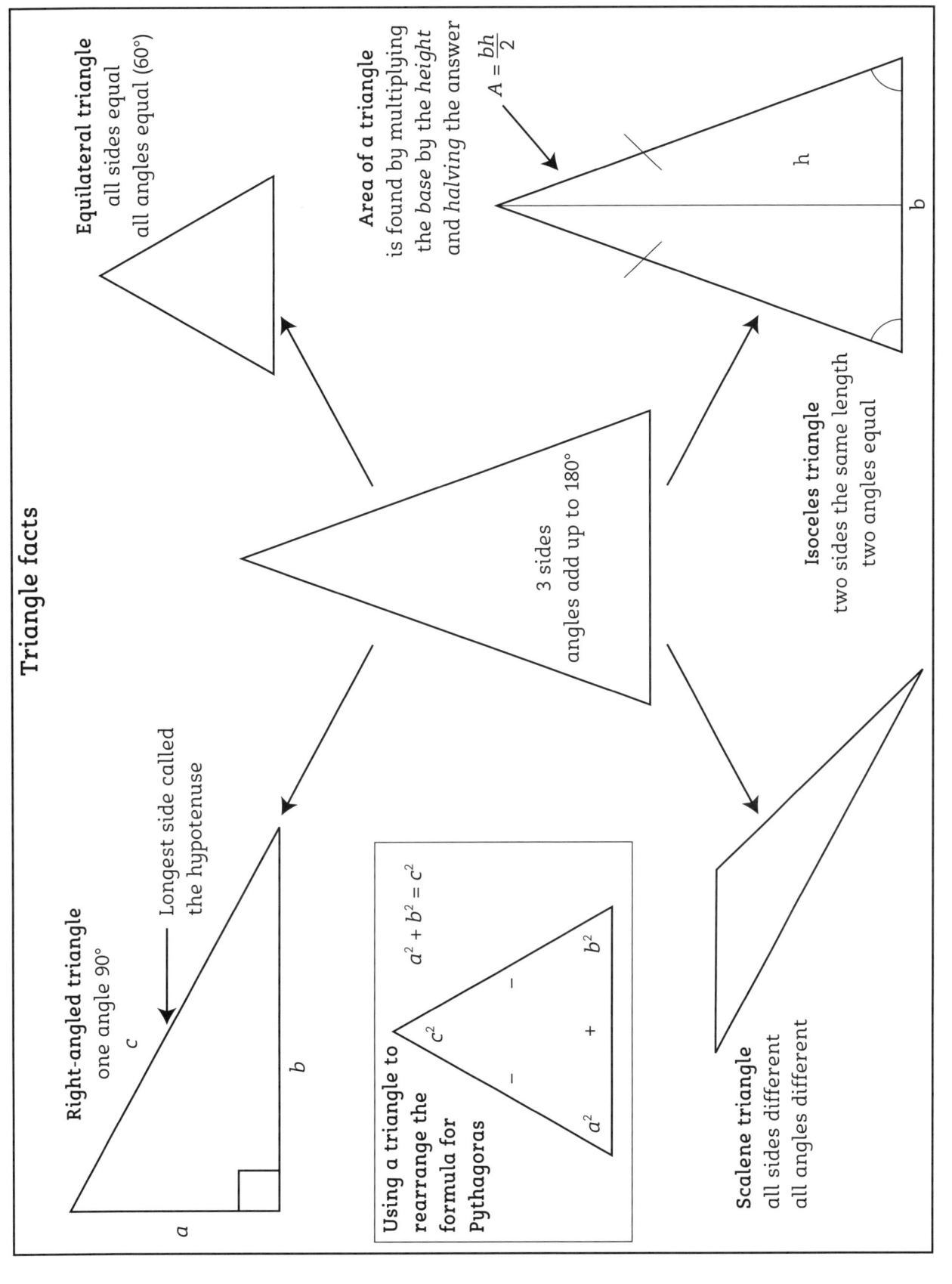

Shape reference cards

Photocopiable resource sheet **12b**

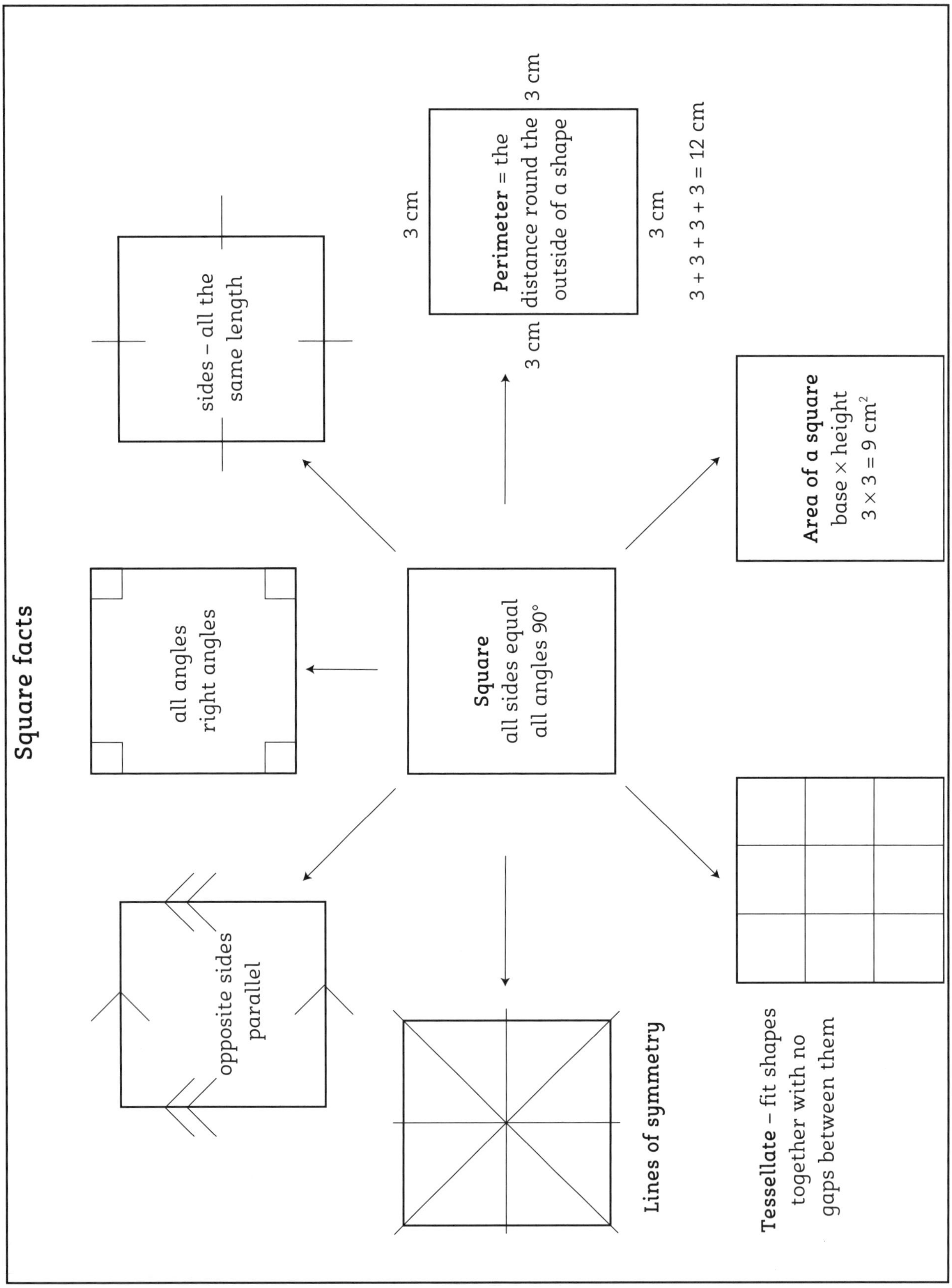
Square facts
Square
all sides equal
all angles 90°
sides – all the same length
Perimeter = the distance round the outside of a shape
3 cm
3 cm
3 cm
3 cm
3 + 3 + 3 + 3 = 12 cm
Area of a square
base × height
3 × 3 = 9 cm²
all angles right angles
opposite sides parallel
Lines of symmetry
Tessellate – fit shapes together with no gaps between them

Amount cards

£5	£7
£10	£16
£20	£27
£25	£51
£50	£87
£75	£123
£100	£520
£105	£621
£110	£999
£125	£705

Reading scales

0	0	0	0	0	0	0
		5	50			100
2	5	10	100	0.5	1	200
		15	150			300
4	10	20	200	1.0	2	400
		25	250			500
6	15	30	300	1.5	3	600
		35	350			700
8	20	40	400	2.0	4	800
		45	450			900
10	25	50	500	2.5	5	1000
		55	550			1100
12	30	60	600	3.0	6	1200
		65	650			1300
14	35	70	700	3.5	7	1400
		75	750			1500
16	40	80	800	4.0	8	1600
		85	850			1700
18	45	90	900	4.5	9	1800
		95	950			1900
20	50	100	1000	5.0	10	2000

Target Maths – Resources Sheets